DELIGHTING IN GOD'S WISDOM

A Study on the Book of Proverbs

by Stacy Davis and Brenda Harris

A Ministry of Calvary Chapel Chester Springs Women in Christ

Delighting in God's Wisdom
A Study on the Book of Proverbs
Part of the Delighting in the Lord Bible Study Series

© Copyright 2018
Calvary Chapel Chester Springs
PO Box 595, Eagle, PA 19480

All rights reserved. No part of this book may be reproduced or transmitted in any form or by any means, electronic or mechanical, including photocopying and recording, or by any information storage or retrieval system, except as may be expressly permitted in writing by the publisher.

ISBN 9781731401342

Unless otherwise indicated, Scripture quotations are from the New King James Version of the Bible.
Copyright © 1982 by Thomas Nelson, Inc. Used by permission.
All rights reserved.

Ministry verse Psalm 27:4 is taken from the Holy Bible, New Living Translation (NLT), copyright © 1996, 2004, 2015 by Tyndale House Foundation. Used by permission of Tyndale House Publishers, Inc., Carol Stream, Illinois 60188. All rights reserved.

Series Cover Design: Melissa Bereda
Cover Photo: Unsplash, Aaron Burden

Printed in the United States of America

"The one thing I ask of the Lord - the thing I seek most - is to live in the house of the Lord all the days of my life, delighting in the Lord's perfections and meditating in his temple." Psalm 27:4

CONTENTS

DELIGHTING IN GOD'S WISDOM

A Study on the Book of Proverbs

Acknowledgments	6
About the Delighting in the Lord Ministry	7-8
Additional Studies	9
About the Authors	10
Introduction	11-12
R.E.A.D. Format	13
Delighting in Your Salvation	14

Week 1   To Know Wisdom
         Proxverbs 1 15-28
         (Queen of Sheba)

Week 2   Wisdom's Value
         Proverbs 2 29-40
         (Ruth)

Week 3   Trust in the Lord
         Proverbs 3 41-51
         (Mary)

Week 4   Stay on Wisdom's Path
         Proverbs 4 52-62
         (Shiphrah and Puah)

Week 5   The Immoral Woman
         Proverbs 5 & 7 63-77
         (Potiphar's Wife)

Week 6   Be Aware of Foolishness
         Proverbs 6 78-90
         (Abigail)

CONTENTS

DELIGHTING IN GOD'S WISDOM

A Study on the Book of Proverbs

Week 7	Wisdom's Invitation Proverbs 8 .... 91-101 (Rahab)	
Week 8	The House They Built: Miss Wisdom and Miss Folly Proverbs 9 .... 102-111 (Lydia)	
Week 9	Family Matters Selected Verses from Proverbs 10-30 .... 112-123 (Rebekah)	
Week 10	Money Matters Selected Verses from Proverbs 10-30 .... 124-135 (Mary of Bethany)	
Week 11	Self-Control Matters Selected Verses from Proverbs 10-30 .... 136-148 (Hannah)	
Week 12	The Mouth Matters Selected Verses from Proverbs 10-30 .... 149-161 (Huldah)	
Week 13	The Wise Woman: MS 31 Proverbs 31 .... 162-173 (Ms. 31)	

Bibliography 174

*"The fear of the LORD
is the beginning of knowledge,
But fools despise
wisdom and instruction."*
Proverbs 1:7

"The one thing I ask of the Lord - the thing I seek most - is to live in the house of the Lord all the days of my life, delighting in the Lord's perfections and meditating in his temple." Psalm 27:4

ACKNOWLEDGMENTS

*"There are diversities of gifts, but the same Spirit.
There are differences of ministries, but the same Lord.
And there are diversities of activities but it is the same God who works all in all.
But the manifestation of the Spirit is given to each one for the profit of all."*
1 Corinthians 12:4-7

Many people with different gifts have come together for the common purpose of sharing God's Word (Matthew 28:19-20). This study is the product of those people and their gifts working together by God's grace. We so appreciate each person and the role they fill.

Pastor Chris Swansen - Theological Editor, Calvary Chapel Chester Springs
Pastor Steven Dorr - Pastoral Support, Calvary Chapel Chester Springs
Carinna LaRocco - Copy Editor
Joan Purdy - Copy Editor
Melissa Bereda - Graphic Designer
Lynn Jensen - Office Support
Chris Good - Photographer

Additionally, we could not fulfill this calling without the love and support of our husbands and children. You are blessings beyond what we could ever express to you. Brenda would also like to thank her mom, Carrie Ferri, for being her example of a Proverbs 31 woman.

From the time God called us to write women's Bible studies, we have considered the call "our reasonable act of service" (Romans 12:1) to Him. We take no personal profit from the sale of the studies, and our families and those involved in the DITL ministry join us in this calling. We pray that these studies will be used by God to draw many deeper into His Word and to the heart of God so that lives and relationships will be transformed by His great power and grace.

With love in Christ,
Stacy and Brenda
Delighting in the Lord Ministry

"The one thing I ask of the Lord - the thing I seek most - is to live in the house of the Lord all the days of my life, delighting in the Lord's perfections and meditating in his temple." Psalm 27:4

ABOUT THE DELIGHTING IN THE LORD MINISTRY

In 2006, Stacy and Brenda were separately called by the Lord to begin ministering to women. Stacy began teaching a Thursday morning Bible study for women at her home church, Calvary Chapel Chester Springs. Each Thursday the ladies met for Bible teaching and small group discussion. Meanwhile, Brenda began a traveling teaching ministry called Life Applications Ministries. Their paths would not cross for two more years. What they did not know was God would form a partnership to fulfill both of their callings, together, in a way neither of them would have foreseen. God was laying the groundwork for the Delighting in the Lord Ministry.

In 2008, Stacy asked Brenda to join the Thursday Bible study as a small group leader. The small group leaders helped with the teaching load, and this became the first year that Stacy and Brenda ministered together.

For the next two years, Brenda and Stacy taught the women who gathered on Thursday mornings using Bible study materials from other Calvary Chapel churches and authors. In 2010, Stacy was diagnosed with invasive breast cancer and Brenda became more hands-on in the women's ministry. It was during that year that God planted the writing seeds in Stacy's and Brenda's hearts. Sensing the Lord's direction to study the book of Matthew the following year, Brenda and Stacy searched for a women's Bible study on Matthew. They found nothing that covered the whole book in a verse-by-verse format, with emphasis on life applications. As Stacy prayed seeking God's direction, God continued speaking to her heart, telling her to "write the study." With much fear and trepidation, Stacy shared this with Brenda who then also began diligently praying for God's direction. As Brenda sought the Lord, He gave her the READ format vision, and then He gave them both Psalm 27:4 which became their ministry verse and foundation:

"The one thing I ask of the Lord, the thing I seek most, is to live in the house of the Lord all my life, *delighting in the Lord's* perfections, and meditating in His temple." (NLT)

After much prayer and with the faith to believe that, since God called them, He would equip them, the *Delighting in the Lord Bible Study Series* was birthed that year.

2011 was spent studying and writing "Delighting in the King," a women's Bible study on the book of Matthew. God brought many key people to support the work, including Pastor Chris Swansen, who read every page of the study for Biblical accuracy. Seeing the need, God also touched the hearts of two women, Carinna LaRocco and Joan Purdy, who became our grammatical editors, reviewing our written words and making sure our studies were without writing errors. He also provided a graphic designer, Melissa Bereda. She has designed all of the logos, covers, and interior pages. Each person God brought to partner with Stacy and Brenda in this ministry has answered God's call on their life to use their gifts for God's glory.

The next year, upon suggestion from the ladies attending the Thursday morning study, the teaching sessions were video recorded and the church began putting all the materials online. These teaching videos are available at www.delightinginthelord.com. Since then, God has used Brenda and Stacy to teach His Word, both in written and spoken form, to the women who gather together on Thursday mornings, as well as to women online, individuals, and those in other study groups and churches.

What began as a simple "Yes, God" became a ministry that teaches God's Word to women, drawing out His truths and life applications. They are simply two women who love Jesus with their whole hearts and lives. They have experienced the power of the cross in their own lives and want to tell others of the saving power and grace of Jesus, so others can live a life of peace and joy in the midst of life's chaos. Even more, so that others can live with hope, knowing their eternal home with Jesus awaits. Since its beginnings in 2011, Stacy and Brenda have written 11 verse-by-verse Bible studies for women. They are humbled hearing testimonies of God's transforming work of the Holy Spirit as women have used these studies to delve into God's word.

"The one thing I ask of the Lord - the thing I seek most - is to live in the house of the Lord all the days of my life, delighting in the Lord's perfections and meditating in his temple." Psalm 27:4

ADDITIONAL STUDIES IN THE DELIGHTING IN THE LORD BIBLE STUDY SERIES

Each verse-by-verse study is inductive and deductive with life application emphasis following the **READ** format: **Receive** God's word, **Experience** God's word, **Act** on God's word, **Delight** in God's word.

Delighting in the King: Matthew *(currently being revised)*

Delighting in God, His Righteousness and Perfect Plan: Romans

Delighting in Being a Child of God: 1,2 & 3 John

Delighting in God's Will and His Provision: Jonah & Nahum

Delighting in the Redeemer, a Love Story: Ruth

Delighting in God's Heart: A study on the Life of David through 1 & 2 Samuel and the Psalms

Delighting in The Holy Spirit: Acts

Delighting in Being a Woman of God: Esther

Delighting in a Life Lived for God: 1 Peter

Delighting in a Life of Triumph: A Study on the Life of Joseph from Genesis 37-50

All studies are available at www.delightinginthelord.com

"The one thing I ask of the Lord - the thing I seek most - is to live in the house of the Lord all the days of my life, delighting in the Lord's perfections and meditating in his temple." Psalm 27:4

ABOUT THE AUTHORS

STACY DAVIS has been teaching women God's Word for over 15 years. She has learned many Biblical truths through difficult trials. Beginning at the age of three with her mother's brain aneurism, to the death of her fourth son and through invasive breast cancer, Stacy's faith has been tried and tested many times over. Her life gives testimony to God's redeeming and transforming power. Stacy teaches with passion the truths of God's Word, desiring to share with all women how to go through everyday struggles victoriously in Jesus Christ. She lives in PA with her husband, Barclay. They have six children.

BRENDA HARRIS's background in education, along with her many years as a classroom teacher, were foundational for the plans God had for her to serve Him. In 2006, she transitioned away from instructing young people how to read literature, and began teaching women they can have a closer walk with the Lord through reading and studying their Bible. She is an enthusiastic teacher who loves a great visual to help demonstrate practical ways to apply God's Word to real life. Brenda lives in PA with her husband, Michael, and their two children.

"The one thing I ask of the Lord - the thing I seek most - is to live in the house of the Lord all the days of my life, delighting in the Lord's perfections and meditating in his temple." Psalm 27:4

INTRODUCTION
DELIGHTING IN GOD'S WISDOM

A Study on the Book of Proverbs

A proverb is a short, concise, often expressive statement that gives advice or expresses a general truth. In the ancient world, proverbs were often used to communicate truths about life. We do the same today, often using short statements to speak nuggets of truth that are easy to remember; "haste makes waste," "a place for everything and everything in its place," and "absence makes the heart grow fonder," just to name a few. Not necessarily meant to be ironclad promises, but rather guides for living a wisdom-filled life.

The Hebrew word for proverb is "mashal." According to Strong's Concordance, it means a rule of conduct to live by expressed in statements and metaphorical comparisons. Using imagery, personifications and contrasts, the book of Proverbs is a poetic book of truths to guide our lives and behavior. But unlike the proverbs made up by man, the book of Proverbs is God's instruction to us in the practical things of life where the fear of God is at the heart of all wisdom. The first comparison we will be given is of the wise and foolish. Many other comparisons follow throughout the book: the humble with the prideful, the rich with the poor, and the self-controlled with the unrestrained. These comparisons in Proverbs may appear simplistic, but are actually quite profound and full of insight. They are bite-sized in nature but loaded with God's truth for life. They are still as applicable today as they were when Solomon first spoke them to the people of Israel.

Proverbs is written in a unique, poetic format unlike many other books of the Bible. The first nine chapters drive home the truth that the foundation for God's wisdom is necessary for successful living. These chapters emphasize how God's wisdom guards you from the traps of life that may detour you away from His commandments and heart. Chapters 10-30 consist of many various topics, and chapter 31 focuses on the Proverbs 31 woman who is called "the virtuous wife." The whole book is filled with wisdom for all areas of life. Wisdom for following God's instructions is available to all of us as we seek to please God with our behaviors and attitudes. If you have been looking for understanding and insights in life, you have come to the right place! Proverbs is the ultimate guide for wisdom and knowledge.

AUTHOR
The authors are King Solomon (1 Kings 4:32), King Hezekiah's committee (Proverbs 25:1), Agur (Proverbs 30) and Lemuel (Proverbs 31).

King Solomon is the primary author. Also known as Jedidiah, Solomon was the second child born to David and Bathsheba. 1 Kings 3:3 tells us that "Solomon loved the LORD," but his heart was divided as he continued sacrificing and burning incense at the high places of Canaanite worship. It was here that the Lord appeared to Solomon in a dream and told him to ask for his heart's desire and it would be given to him. Solomon asked God for an understanding, discerning heart to judge the people justly, and to know good from evil. God gave Solomon what he asked for as well as riches and honor. God told Solomon that "there shall not be anyone like you among the kings all your days" (1 Kings 3:13). He was the wisest king that ever lived; even so his worldly desires took his heart away from God. If the heart is not guarded, even the wisest person can fall.

Solomon also wrote Ecclesiastes and Song of Solomon.

PURPOSE
The purpose of Proverbs is given in Proverbs 1:7. "The fear of the LORD is the beginning of knowledge, but fools despise wisdom and instruction." The book was written from the perspective of a father writing to his son. He gives instruction on how to be wise to help his son, as well as the reader, to live a life that pleases God.

DATE
Approximately 950-700 B.C.

WEEKLY WRITTEN LESSONS
This study on Proverbs is broken into 13 weeks. We will study the first nine chapters verse by verse; Proverbs 10-30 will be studied topically; and the final week will examine Proverbs 31. We have selected a few broad topics for you to focus on from chapters 10-30, including family matters, money matters, self-control matters and mouth matters. We will study verses across these chapters thematically, and examine how we can apply them to everyday life. The final week concludes with a verse-by-verse study of the virtuous and wise woman of chapter 31. For each of the 13 weeks, we have picked a woman from the Bible to highlight the wisdom being given in Proverbs. You will learn about each woman and what makes her either a wise or unwise example of the principles being studied.

Each week you will only go through the R.E.A.D. format once in your homework. You may choose to do the homework in one sitting or in many; it is totally up to you. You should plan on about 60-90 minutes to complete the whole week's study. We highly encourage you to spend the time in God's Word answering these questions and digging into the text for yourself. You will find that your time investment will be given back to you deeply for your spiritual growth.

"The one thing I ask of the Lord - the thing I seek most - is to live in the house of the Lord all the days of my life, delighting in the Lord's perfections and meditating in his temple." Psalm 27:4

FORMAT: "READ" THE BIBLE

*The format for this study follows the acronym **READ**: Read the Bible.*

RECEIVING God's Word

1. **Open in Prayer:** Before reading God's word, you need to prepare your heart to receive from Him what He has for you.
- During this time of prayer, confess any sin that may be present in your life.
- Ask God to open "the eyes of your heart" (Eph 1:18) so you can hear from Him what He wants to communicate to you.
- Thank Him in advance for what He will do!
2. **Receiving:** Read the scripture text given.

EXPERIENCING God's Word

This is where you will dive into the Bible and the daily chapter/verses. You'll be answering questions that lead you through the text by first observing the details, and then focusing on the connections within the text to the bigger picture. At other times, you may be investigating other verses from the whole counsel of God, and then drawing some Biblical conclusions from what you have read. There may be several "experiences" drawn from the text.

ACTING on God's Word

In this part of the study you will be applying these verses to your life. We read in Hebrews 4:12 that God's word is "living and powerful, and sharper than any two-edged sword, piercing even to the division of soul and spirit, and of joints and marrow, and is a discerner of the thoughts and intents of the heart." Therefore, as you are studying, God will be speaking to your heart and life. We will be encouraging you to look at applications, but God may have other things He is speaking to your heart. We pray you hear directly from Him. As you listen to the Lord speak to your heart, may He show you what steps He desires you take as you walk out your faith in Him.

DELIGHTING in God's Word

In this final section you will reflect upon what you have learned and offer up your praise and thanksgiving to the Lord. As you close out your daily time, may you truly find that He is the delight of your heart! He fills like no other and nothing else can. And as you "delight yourself in the LORD" He will give you the desires of your heart (Psalm 37:4); because after studying His word, your desires and His should be the same. Through your time in God's word, may you grow more and more into His image. You will be asked to record a verse (or as many as you want!) that stood out to you from the text, and then memorize it if you so desire.

"The one thing I ask of the Lord - the thing I seek most - is to live in the house of the Lord all the days of my life, delighting in the Lord's perfections and meditating in his temple." Psalm 27:4

DELIGHTING IN MY SALVATION

If you have never accepted Jesus Christ as your Savior but desire to take that step of faith, all you need to do is:

Recognize that God loves you!
"For God so loved the world that He gave His only begotten Son, that whoever believes in Him should not perish but have everlasting life." (John 3:16)

"But God demonstrates His own love toward us, in that while we were still sinners, Christ died for us." (Romans 5:8)

Admit that you are a sinner.
For all have sinned and fall short of the glory of God." (Romans 3:23)

"As it is written: 'There is none righteous, no, not one;' " (Romans 3:10)

Recognize Jesus Christ as being God's only remedy for sin.
"For the wages of sin is death, but the gift of God is eternal life in Christ Jesus our Lord." (Romans 6:23)

"But as many as received Him, to them He gave the right to become children of God, to those who believe in His name:" (John 1:12)

"For I delivered to you first of all that which I also received: that Christ died for our sins according to the Scriptures, and that He was buried, and that He rose again the third day according to the Scriptures." (1 Corinthians 15:3-4)

Receive Jesus Christ as your personal Savior!
"If you confess with your mouth the Lord Jesus and believe in your heart that God has raised Him from the dead, you will be saved." (Romans 10:9)

Prayer is simply "talking with God." Right now, go to God in prayer and ask Christ to be your Savior. You might pray something like this:

"Lord Jesus, I need You. I confess that I am a sinner and that You paid the penalty for my sin through Your death on the cross. I believe that You died for my sins and were raised from the dead. I ask You to come into my heart, take control of my life, and make me the kind of person that You want me to be. Thank You for coming into my life as You promised." Amen.

If you have prayed to accept Christ as your Savior, please tell someone today! Share this exciting news with a close Christian friend, your small group leader or your pastor. They will be thrilled to encourage you in your faith and your decision to follow Jesus!

Delighting in God's Wisdom

"The one thing I ask of the Lord - the thing I seek most - is to live in the house of the Lord all the days of my life, delighting in the Lord's perfections and meditating in his temple." Psalm 27:4

WEEK 1
TO KNOW WISDOM

Proverbs 1

His reputation was growing quickly as the wisest man, not only in Jerusalem but everywhere. Story upon story spread of this king and his wisdom; how he executed judgment, and had discernment and knowledge in every situation. As she sat on the throne in Ethiopia, the queen of Sheba couldn't believe the reports she was hearing. It pricked her heart. His wisdom was desirable. How wonderful it would be to truly have wisdom for every situation and aspect of life. She wondered how it was possible that a man could have such knowledge and understanding, and that it came from God. She had to see him for herself. Her skepticism was kindled. She would test his wisdom. She was sure she could stump him with her hard questions. Calling to her attendants to prepare for the journey, she had her assistants and advisors gather many valuables together to bring to the king. It would be a long journey, but even 1,400 miles wouldn't hinder her quest to see this wise ruler in Jerusalem and maybe, just maybe, gain some of his wisdom.

They entered Jerusalem and made their way to King Solomon's home. She was overcome with all she saw around his palace. Her eyes could scarcely take it in; the food at his tables, his servants, their clothes, and their happy dispositions. Astonished at what she saw, the queen of Sheba wanted to see more but knew he was expecting her. Her heart beat rapidly as she was led to him. Everything that was in her heart, she asked of him. Question after question; he had the answers. Nothing was too hard for King Solomon to explain. Who was this man? More questions came spilling out of her mouth until she confessed saying, "King Solomon, your fame exceeds the fame of which I heard. It is a true report, but I didn't believe it until I came and saw it with my own eyes. Blessed be the Lord your God" (2 Chronicles 9:6,8; 1 Kings 10:7,9). As she gushed with praise and blessing, not only for Solomon but also for his God, the queen of Sheba gave King Solomon an abundance of spices, gold, and precious stones in thanksgiving and gratitude. As she turned to leave, Solomon asked her, "What can I give you?" She wondered, "How is it that he wants to give me gifts?" All that she asked from Solomon, he gave her, even more than she had given him.

Oh girls, this is God's heart for us regarding wisdom. Does your heart cry out for wisdom? Have you seen others walk wisely, desiring what they have? I (Stacy) think so often we search for wisdom in all the wrong places. The world's answers entice us, pretending to hold the right answers. We sometimes get caught off guard letting them give us wisdom instead of turning to the One wise, life giver – God Himself. He is wisdom. Just as the queen of Sheba could not believe a wise Godly life was possible, we too, often doubt it. The queen of Sheba sought wisdom from Solomon. She opened her heart and received all he had to offer and then poured out her life through gifts to him. He, in return, gave her more than she had given him.

That's what God desires to do with us. He speaks; asking us to come, to listen, to receive. It starts with salvation and spills over into all of life. When we receive wisdom and understanding from the deep things of His heart, we know how to respond to life in a way that honors Him. It brings peace to our hearts, and we can't help but give Him thanks. He then gives us even more of Himself.

The book of Proverbs is unlike any other book in the Bible. Most of it was written by King Solomon during his 40-year reign as king of Israel. Solomon writes to us as a father speaks to his child; giving instruction, encouragement and cautions. He was known as the wisest man to ever live. And yet, even as the wisest man, his heart was divided as he allowed his sinful desires to lure him away from God. Living in the Canaanite culture, Solomon got caught up in their lifestyle of idolatry. 1 Kings 11 tells us that, "King Solomon loved many foreign women and clung to them in love." This would be his downfall. He allowed the foreign women to turn his heart away from God. In God's righteous judgment of sin, He took the kingdom from Solomon. His life is a representation to us of one whose life began seeking God's wisdom but failed to listen to it when he was old. His life ended in sorrow.

It is from these life experiences, under the power of the Holy Spirit, that Solomon writes the book of Proverbs. It is an instruction book for us, but it is also a love letter from God. He loves us so much that He wants us to have all that He has. He wants us to be wise. He wants us to know how to handle any situation that He allows. "Take heed and listen," Solomon says. Wisdom is speaking. Wisdom is calling. Wisdom is available. This is God's heart for us. Will we listen and readily receive all that wisdom has to offer us? I'm listening, are you?

RECEIVING God's Word

Open in Prayer
Read Proverbs 1

 EXPERIENCING God's Word

Experience 1: Know Wisdom - Proverbs 1:1-9

Read Proverbs 1:1-6. It is important to have an objective when giving instruction. The book of Proverbs is a tutorial on Godly wisdom and a guide to successfully navigating life's circumstances. Solomon is the author of Proverbs, and under the inspiration of the Holy Spirit, he gives us six objectives for writing this book. Fill in the blanks below:

a. Proverbs 1:2 "To know _____ and _____"

b. Proverbs 1:2 "To perceive the _____ of _____"

c. Proverbs 1:3 "To receive the instruction of _____, _____, _____, and _____"

d. Proverbs 1:4 "To give _____ to the _____"

e. Proverbs 1:4 "To [give] the young man _____ and _____"

f. Proverbs 1:6 "To understand a _____ and an _____, the words of the _____ and their _____."

2. The book of Proverbs is like a "how-to book" on wisdom. Therefore, it is important to take a moment and understand the definition of the word wisdom more fully. The word wisdom in verse 2 is chokmah (H2451) and is taken from the word chakam (H2449), which means to act wisely and skillfully, making the right choices at the necessary times. Solomon couples wisdom with instruction. The word instruction in verse 2 is musar (H4148), and it means discipline, chastening and correction. We are told we need to know wisdom and instruction. Based on these definitions, how are both wisdom and instruction necessary for wise living? How do these two things work together?

3. Wisdom can often be misunderstood as only a process of the intellect. Look at the verbs Solomon uses in defining our purpose on the study of wisdom. Would you agree that wisdom is purely intellectual? Why or why not?

4. According to verse 5, we are given instructions about a wise man. Summarize the instructions in your own words.

5. Verse 7a is the theme verse to the entire book of Proverbs. It tells us that the knowledge of spiritual things starts with the fear of the Lord. This type of fear speaks to revering God as the Supreme Author and Authority over all things. This type of fear is not an emotional fear of doom but, rather, one that recognizes and respects who God is and who you are because of Him. Explain why the fear of God is the beginning of knowledge.

   a. A reverential fear of God is understood when we acknowledge our sin before God. Once we recognize we are sinners and the only payment for our sin is through God's son, Jesus Christ, and His death on the cross, we can repent and receive His forgiveness. Salvation is given when we confess our sins and put our faith in Jesus Christ by asking Him to be our Savior. If you have never made this decision, we invite you to turn to the introductory pages and read "Delighting in My Salvation." Please let someone know if you decide to take this step and write the date of your decision below.

6. In verse 7b, the wise person is contrasted with a fool which we will see throughout the book of Proverbs. The word "fool" means nabal (H5036), keciyl (H3684), and eviyl (H191). Nabal means a person who lacks spiritual perception. Keciyl means someone who has a dull and closed mind. Eviyl means arrogant, flippant and mentally dull. Explain how all of these descriptions are rooted in self.

19   Week 1: To Know Wisdom

7. As we study chapters 1-7 of Proverbs, we will see the phrase "my son" used fifteen times. (This same phrase reappears in chapters 19-31.) The advice which follows the phrase "my son" could be considered advice from a God-fearing father to a child (son or daughter) spoken with both urgency and love. The first of these "my son" phrases begins in Proverbs 1:8. Read Proverbs 1:8-9. When reading these verses, keep in mind that graceful ornaments and chains refer to adornments you would wear. What is the counsel the father gives his son, and if he follows the advice of the father, how will it affect the son's life?

    a. Solomon is saying the fear of the Lord needs to come first, and admonishes his son to honor his parents next. Read Colossians 3:20 and Ephesians 6:1. What commands are given in these verses, and how do they correlate with Solomon's advice in verse 7?

    b. Why is it important to understand that the Godly authorities in our life are a source of God's wisdom?

Delighting in God's Wisdom

Experience 2: Wisdom's Counterfeit; Foolishness - Proverbs 1:10-19

1. Read Proverbs 1:10-15. The father cautions his son to be aware of how sinners will want to entice him to do evil. How do you see this temptation offered in these verses? List the phrases below.

    a. The father gives an admonition in verse 10 regarding sin. What is it and why?

    b. In verse 8 the father tells the son to "hear" him. In verse 10 the father says, "Do not consent," and in verse 15 he says, "Do not walk with evil." Do you see a progression of the will here? If so, describe its impact toward wise or foolish living.

2. Read Proverbs 1:16-19. From these verses, how is the path of the sinner described? What is the end result of walking this way?

Experience 3: Wisdom Calls; Will You Listen? - Proverbs 1:20-33

1. Read Proverbs 1:20-33. In these verses wisdom is personified as a woman. Answer the questions below based on these verses.

    a. In verses 20-21 wisdom calls out to anyone who will hear. Does wisdom discriminate? Explain.

    b. How does wisdom, as seen in these verses, reflect the heart of God?

    c. In verse 22 wisdom speaks. She begins by addressing three groups of people. List the three groups below and why each disregards what wisdom offers.

    d. Verse 23 starts with the word "turn". Why is turning away from sin so essential to anyone who wants to follow after wisdom's call? What encouragement does she offer for the person who will receive her?

e. How does the fool show his foolishness in verses 24-27?

f. It appears the fool is desperate for wisdom in verses 28-30. Read Romans 1:18-25. How do these verses help explain why wisdom does not respond to the fool asking for help?

g. Using verses 31-32, describe the path of the fool and the way of destruction.

h. Read verse 33. What does wisdom offer to the person who heeds her instruction?

2. Read 1 Kings 11:1-13. Solomon's choices during his life exemplify what we have just studied.

a. How was Solomon lured into sin?

b. How is his heart described toward God?

c. How would his choices impact his own plea to his son in the book of Proverbs?

Experience 4: The Queen of Sheba
Read 1 Kings 10:1-13

1. The queen of Sheba went to King Solomon and asked him questions. Reread verses 1-5. What was the substance of her questions and why did she go to him?

2. From verses 6-7, what had she heard about King Solomon and why might she have questioned the reports about him?

3. In verse 8 the queen of Sheba made an observation about King Solomon's servants. How does wisdom seem to affect the attitude of other people?

4. In verses 9-13, who does the queen of Sheba credit for King Solomon's wisdom and how is Godly wisdom made evident? How do the queen of Sheba and King Solomon respond?

5. From these verses, what do you observe about how the queen of Sheba identified true wisdom?

ACTING on God's Word

An accumulation of knowledge without the ability to apply it seems like a worthless pursuit. I (Brenda) desire to apply what I read in my Bible to my daily life in practical ways so I can know God better, follow His commands and enjoy my relationship with Him. Proverbs gives us many bite-sized chunks of knowledge in every chapter. So much so, that it can be a bit overwhelming at the sheer volume of wisdom contained in the overall book. However, when we arrive at the Acting portion of the study, Stacy and I would like to present you with just a handful of proverbs that you can insert into your present-day life. Let's take a look at a few and see how God would have you apply wisdom's call.

1. Proverbs 1:7 says, "The fear of the Lord is the beginning of knowledge. But fools despise wisdom and instruction." How does this proverb challenge your current level of reverential fear for God and your genuine desire to be full of His wisdom?

2. Proverbs 1:8a says, "My son, hear the instruction of your father, and do not forsake the law of your mother." When learning new things, there needs to be a certain amount of humility on the part of the learner. They must recognize their need for additional knowledge and understanding. Take a moment and admit before God that you do not know what God knows, and you desire His wisdom to understand what He wants you to learn from the book of Proverbs. (This can be done silently, or you may write out your prayer.)

3. Proverbs 1:10 says, "My son, if sinners entice you, do not consent." Are there areas of sin in your life which you have allowed? Take a few moments to search your heart and ask God for His forgiveness. (This can be done silently, or you may write out your prayer.)

4. Proverbs 1:23 says, "Turn at my rebuke; surely I will pour out my spirit on you; I will make my words known to you." We must turn away from our sin. When we do this, the Lord will cleanse us and help us to begin again with the ability to hear Him without sin hindering us. How would you like God to pour out His Spirit upon you through your time studying Proverbs?

5. Proverbs 1:33 says, "But whoever listens to me will dwell safely, and will be secure without fear of evil." There is an abundant life available for those who know God's wisdom. Write below any areas where you are lacking wisdom and commit these area(s) to the Lord in prayer, trusting that He will answer you.

 **DELIGHTING** in God's Word

Reflecting back on our chapter, how has the Lord prompted you to pray?

Write a verse from the chapter that God has spoken to your heart.

Close in Prayer

"The one thing I ask of the Lord - the thing I seek most - is to live in the house of the Lord all the days of my life, delighting in the Lord's perfections and meditating in his temple." Psalm 27:4

WEEK 2
WISDOM'S VALUE

Proverbs 2

It had been a hard ten years in Moab. The famine had devastated much of the land. Sorrow permeated the air at the home of Naomi, Ruth, and Orpah. So much loss. First Naomi's husband, Elimelech, died and now the husbands of Ruth and Orpah have died. Naomi had made the decision to travel back to Bethlehem after she heard that the Lord had provided for the people by giving them bread. Ruth, clinging to Naomi as she got ready to leave, couldn't let her go alone. Making an affirmation of faith in God, Ruth was ready to forsake everything to follow God, even if that meant relocating and remaining single until she died. Knowing that life with Naomi was the wise decision, she said to Naomi, "Your people shall be my people, and your God, my God" (Ruth 1:16b).

Life was hard in Bethlehem for the two widows. Ruth quickly knew that she needed to find a field and glean for food, as this was the provision for the poor given in the Law of Moses. She wisely shared this with Naomi who gave her blessing. Standing in the field under the hot sun and feeling tired from a full day of reaping, she saw him coming. He passed through the field greeting the reapers saying, "The Lord be with you." They respectfully answered, "The Lord bless you." Boaz noticed Ruth. She was new to the fields. He also had heard about her and all she had done for Naomi. She had made an impression on him. Addressing her, Boaz gave clear instructions for her protection and her provision. He extended grace to her that day by giving her more than she could have imagined. She wisely listened to all he said and obeyed his directions. The months passed, and Ruth enjoyed the blessing of abundance from Boaz's hand.

From the days in Moab, Naomi had been asking God to give Ruth and Orpah rest and security. She had prayed this for years, and now she was seeing God's answer and provision. God made the answer clear. Ruth listened intently while Naomi shared her wisdom. Naomi told her Boaz was a close relative and had the responsibility of marrying her. A plan was set in motion to make Ruth's intent known. That night Boaz not only received Ruth's request by calling her blessed, but he also praised her for her righteous and Godly lifestyle. This life she never thought possible was hers; Boaz would be her husband, and she would be his wife. After years of treasuring God's commands, inclining her ear to His wisdom and seeking God, He met her in her need. He was her shield and her guard. Discretion preserved her. She was walking in God's goodness, and boy did it feel good. Her heart swelled with thanksgiving that day as she took Boaz to be her husband.

In Proverbs 2 we'll hear God reach across the pages of Scripture and encourage each of us to seek His wisdom, to incline our ears to Him, and receive all that He has to say. There is great value, eternal value, in all He has for us. Seek Him and search for the wisdom He alone can give for your specific life. Maybe you are looking at your life thinking, "It won't get better." Maybe you've waited and waited for God to give you His next steps, and you're still waiting. Go to His Word and search Him out. Solomon tells us, "The LORD gives wisdom." "He stores up sound wisdom" for those who walk uprightly before Him (Proverbs 2:6-7). The knowledge of God is there for the child of God who fears Him. I (Stacy) pray that as you study Proverbs 2, God will meet you in your need. He will reveal His wisdom to you and, like Ruth, you will enjoy all the benefits of walking in God's goodness and wisdom.

RECEIVING God's Word

Open in Prayer
Read Proverbs 2

EXPERIENCING God's Word

Experience 1: Seeking Wisdom - Proverbs 2:1-5

1. Read Proverbs 2:1-4 and answer the following questions:

    a. Solomon begins with another "my son" phrase which is followed by the word "if." He gives us many verbs in these verses. What are they? Define them in your own words and describe how they are all needed in our pursuit of Godly wisdom.

Delighting in God's Wisdom

b. How is wisdom described?

c. List the body parts that are included in these verses. Why is each part significant in our pursuit of Godly wisdom?

d. How do these verses imply that effort is needed on our part? Explain.

2. Here Solomon is talking about a steadfast, purposeful pursuit of God. In order to learn from Him, we must spend time in His Word. Explain the difference between studying God's Word and reading about God's Word.

3. Look up the following verses that speak to God's pursuit of us. What do you learn?

- Jeremiah 29:13-14

- Matthew 18:12-14

- John 4:23

Experience 2: Benefits of Wisdom - Proverbs 2:6-13a

1. Read Proverbs 2:6-9. Verse 9 begins with the word "then." It was the completion to the if/then statement that began in verse 1. What do you learn about God from verses 6-9 and what He offers the person who is in pursuit of Him?

    a. Read verse 9. This "then" statement tells us we will gain understanding. Why does understanding of righteousness, justice, equity and good paths come from our pursuit of God?

2. In Proverbs 2:10 we hear about the effect wisdom has upon someone when it enters their heart. Describe it.

3. Sometimes with an instruction manual such as Proverbs, our tendency can be to create a list of desired behaviors and then act on them legalistically. In Proverbs 2:10 Solomon makes mention of the heart as the central system needed for wisdom. Explain the difference between the action that comes from the heart versus the action that comes from a "to do" list. Why does instruction need to penetrate our hearts?

4. Read the following verses about the heart and record what you learn next to the verse.

- Psalm 26:2

- Matthew 15:18

- Proverbs 4:23

5. Read Proverbs 2:11-13. Describe how God can protect the person who has hidden wisdom in their heart.

Experience 3: The Way of Darkness and the Way of Goodness - Proverbs 2:13b-22

1. Read Proverbs 2:13b-15. There is a description of an evil person given who is walking in the way of darkness. Describe them based on these verses.

   a. From what you have studied, how does wisdom guard you against this type of person and why do we need to be guarded?

2. In verses 16-19 we meet an immoral woman. Describe her below.

Delighting in God's Wisdom

    a. From what you have studied, how does wisdom guard you?

3. How does the wisdom of God differ from the wisdom of the world when confronted with evil people and immoral people?

4. Read Proverbs 2:20-22. In these verses we see God's heart toward the person walking in the way of goodness. How does this person walk?

    a. In verse 21 how does God bless the person who walks in the way of goodness?

5. In verse 23 God's judgment toward an evil person is given. Why do you think His judgment is so severe?

a. Read 1 Kings 11:9-13. How was God's judgment executed toward Solomon in light of his heart and choices?

Experience 4: Ruth
Read Ruth

1. Read Ruth 1:1-22. Ruth and Orpah are married to Naomi's sons. Naomi's husband dies, along with her two sons, leaving the women as widows. When Naomi tells her daughters-in-law that she is going back to her hometown of Bethlehem, how does Ruth observe Naomi's wisdom in this decision and demonstrate wisdom herself?

2. In chapter 2, Ruth acts wisely by taking advantage of the growing season and the provision given through the Law of Moses, which allows the poor to glean grain from the farmers' fields. She wisely picks Boaz's fields. Read Ruth 2:1-23. How did Ruth and Naomi benefit from Boaz's wisdom?

3. In chapter 3, Ruth acts wisely toward Boaz. Read Ruth 3:1-18. Describe her wisdom in her interaction with Boaz.

4. Read Ruth 4:1-21. How was Ruth's future affected by surrounding herself with wisdom, recognizing wisdom, and acting in wisdom?

A ACTING on God's Word

The pursuit of wisdom reminds me a little bit like writing a research paper. However, I'm (Brenda) not talking about writing a research paper today, but rather what it was like for me when I attended college. Back then, in order to write a research paper, it began with a trip to the library where I would search through the card catalog to locate books that might be on the shelf. Next, I would visit the dreaded microfilm room to examine any newspaper or magazine articles that might aid my understanding. Finally, I would swing past the Encyclopedia Britannica shelf and see if, on the off-chance, there was anything additional to glean there about my topic. The process of gathering the materials to research was such a laborious process, but it did not deter me from my end goal. I believed the final product, as well as the grade I hoped to receive, was worth the effort.

In Proverbs 2, Solomon encourages his son to pursue wisdom with all his might because there is great value in Godly wisdom. He tells him it will take effort on his part; it will require something from him; but in the end, it will be worth it. Let's take a look at Proverbs 2:1-4 and see how we can apply these verses to our life.

1. Proverbs 2:1 says, "My son, if you receive my words, and treasure my commands within you." In order to receive wisdom, we must receive the words of our Father as well as treasure them. In what ways do you demonstrate that you both want to receive His words and that you also treasure them? Do you struggle in doing this? If so, how?

2. Proverbs 2:2 says, "So that you incline your ear to wisdom and apply your heart to understanding." Often wisdom can be found in a book, but other times it can come from the voice of a Godly and discerning person. How do you practice inclining your ears for wisdom?

    a. In what ways are you tuning out things that are not wise? Is this easy or difficult? Explain.

3. Proverbs 2:3 says, "Yes, if you cry out for discernment, and lift up your voice for understanding." When was the last time you literally cried out for God's wisdom in your prayer life?

   a. Do you find that sometimes it requires a challenging set of circumstances before you cry out to God in this manner? Explain.

4. Proverbs 2:4 says, "If you seek her [wisdom] as silver, and search for her as for hidden treasures." God wants to give us His wisdom. Why do you think Solomon compared searching for wisdom like searching for hidden treasures? Can you relate to this comparison? Why or why not?

5. Proverbs 2:5 says, "Then you will understand the fear of the Lord and find the knowledge of God." I love this verse. God tells us that when we search for Him, He will be found by us. It might take work and determination but, in the end, we will find the wisdom we seek. Close in prayer thanking God that He will show you the wisdom He alone knows.

 **DELIGHTING** in God's Word

Reflecting back on our chapter, how has the Lord prompted you to pray?

Write a verse from the chapter that God has spoken to your heart.

Close in Prayer

"The one thing I ask of the Lord - the thing I seek most - is to live in the house of the Lord all the days of my life, delighting in the Lord's perfections and meditating in his temple." Psalm 27:4

WEEK 3
TRUST IN THE LORD
Proverbs 3

Mary groped around in the darkness collecting any items she would need to travel. It was the middle of the night and she was packing with great haste to flee Bethlehem. What a day it had been! The house had been full after the arrival of three unexpected guests from the East. As the men entered, they explained how they had followed a star a long way until it miraculously stood still over their home. They were pursuing a star which they believed would lead them to the "King of the Jews." They were overjoyed when they met Jesus and fell down to worship Him. Further, these unique men brought costly treasures of gold, frankincense, and myrrh as gifts for their family.

How many more ways would the Lord convey to her that Jesus was the Messiah? How many times would He prove to her that the wisdom which had been imparted to her was true and divine? Life was certainly sending her many startling surprises which caused her to trust and rely on Him deeply. However, this newest twist, escaping to Egypt in the middle of the night, seemed incomprehensible. Joseph had awoken her abruptly just moments prior explaining that an angel of the Lord had appeared to him in a dream saying, "Arise and take the young Child and His mother; flee to Egypt and stay there until I bring you word, for Herod will seek the young Child to destroy Him." Questions filled her mind. How long would they be in Egypt before it would be safe for them to return? Where would they live? Would Joseph find work easily? So many questions but so few answers; however, knowing God had given her husband this marvelous, wise revelation, she embraced the decision to leave. She would have to trust that God would guide and protect them, knowing He alone knew their future. (Matthew 2:1-15)

In Proverbs 3, Solomon expresses the importance of trusting God. When we put our faith in God, He can protect us from unwanted circumstances which could bring about harm and, at the same time, develop our trust in Him. Mary, the mother of Jesus, trusted the instruction her husband received from the Lord to depart from Bethlehem so they would be safe from Herod's murderous plan. Similarly, in Proverbs 3 we find Solomon encouraging his son to trust in the Lord with all his heart so he would "not be afraid of sudden terror" (v. 25). God is worthy of our trust. May that trust in Him be multiplied as we study Proverbs 3.

R RECEIVING God's Word

Open in Prayer
Read Proverbs 3

E EXPERIENCING God's Word

Experience 1: Trust in the Lord - Proverbs 3:1-12

1. Verse 1 begins again with the endearing greeting of "my son." Solomon has words of encouragement to give us about trusting in God. Read verses 1-4. List the 6 commands Solomon gives us (his son).

    a. What benefits come from following these commands?

2. Proverbs 3:5-6 may be some of the most well-known verses in all of the Bible. What does faith look like according to these verses? What does it not look like?

Delighting in God's Wisdom

3. The word "acknowledge" in the Hebrew is "yada" (H3045). It means to know with intimate knowledge or from experience. How does this definition help you to understand verse 6? What does it mean to "yada" God?

4. In verse 6 we are told that God will direct our paths or make them straight when we follow his commands in the preceding verses. So often we need to know God's will and direction for our lives. How do verses 1-6 help us build our trust in God, especially when the circumstances in our lives might be confusing and direction seems unknown? Explain.

5. Read verse 7-8. Explain what it means to be wise in your own eyes. What is the root sin behind this behavior?

   a. How will fearing and trusting God bring strength to the inner person?

6. Read verses 9-12. In these verses you will find two areas of life where your faith may be tried and tested. What are these two areas and why do you think these are areas where we can be tempted to be wise in our own eyes?

   a. Read verses 9-10. Here we are given a command. Explain how we can honor God with our possessions. What does it mean to give the first fruits to the Lord from our increases?

   b. Read Proverbs 3:11-12 and Hebrews 12:7-10. What do you learn about God's love and His reasons for chastening?

Experience 2: The Immeasurable Wisdom of God - Proverbs 3:13-20

1. Proverbs 3:13 characterizes the person who finds wisdom and gains understanding. This person is described as someone who is happy. The word "happy" in Hebrew is "esher" (H835), and it means blessed. When you encounter the word "her" or "she" in Proverbs 3:13-20, you can substitute the word "wisdom." In verses 14-18 Solomon lists the blessings that come from finding wisdom. Write them below.

Delighting in God's Wisdom

    a. The word "happy" is a description given again in verse 18. What is the wise person doing to experience this blessing in their life? How is this verse tied to Proverbs 3:1-4?

2. Read Proverbs 3:19-20. What do we learn about the magnitude of God's wisdom and how should this effect our trust in Him?

Experience 3: Do not be afraid - Proverbs 3:21-26

1. In verse 21 we read Solomon telling his son to not let "them" depart from his eyes. The word "them" is referring to the wisdom and discretion he has obtained from God. Read Proverbs 3:21-22. Why are wisdom and discretion so important in your relationship with God and for your life?

2. Read Proverbs 3:23-26. What connection is Solomon making between wisdom, discretion and fear?

Experience 4: Love your neighbor - Proverbs 3:27-35

1. In Proverbs 3:27-31 Solomon seems to take a turn by focusing on our treatment of other people. How are we instructed to treat other people?

2. Read verses 32-33. What is God's heart toward those who are wicked?

3. In verse 33 Solomon tells us that God blesses the home of the just. Read Hebrews 10:38. How is the just person commanded to live?

    a. How does this enable you to deal with difficult people as well as demonstrate your trust in God to others?

    b. Read verses 34-35. How does God view pride and humility? How are they tied to wisdom and foolishness?

    c. Read Jeremiah 9:23-24. How does this verse summarize what we learned in Proverbs 3?

Experience 5: Mary
Read Matthew 2:1-15

1. Read Matthew 2:1-4. Why were King Herod and all Jerusalem troubled and what did King Herod do in response?

2. In Matthew 2:5-6 the wise men tell King Herod of a prophecy concerning Jesus who is "King of the Jews." What did the prophecy, quoted from Micah 5:2, say about Jesus?

3. Read Matthew 2:7-13. Herod had a plan that he was devising in secret and deceptive ways. What was his plan and how did he deceive the wise men?

   a. How did the wise men learn of Herod's plan?

   b. How were Mary and Joseph made aware of Herod's plan?

4. From verses 14-15 describe Mary and Joseph's escape. How might this have been a test of their faith as well as a real-life example of Proverbs 3:5-6?

ACTING on God's Word

This past year our family joined the boating community. My (Stacy's) husband grew up spending much time on a lake in southern Virginia water skiing, jet skiing and swimming. For years he longed to share his love of the water, as well as boating, with our children. What a joy it has been this summer spending family time on the Chesapeake Bay. One week our boating plans included a long boat ride to a little village on an inlet. Being new to the Chesapeake waters, we weren't sure how long the round-trip boat ride would take. We found ourselves traveling back to the marina as the sun was setting and darkness descending. It is a little unsettling being on the water in the dark. The shoreline seems to disappear into the shadows, and the waters become black like the night sky. Thankfully, my husband is an experienced boater. I trusted his abilities in the midst of uncertainty. I asked him some questions about how he navigates in the dark, knowing his wisdom would settle my heart.

In his gentle and reassuring way, he told me that in the dark you have to trust the channel markers that are illuminated at night. One has a red flashing light and the other a green flashing light. He went on to say that our boating direction determined which light marker was to be on either side of the channel. Those lights keep you safe. The only problem is they are spaced pretty far apart. As I stood next to him while he steered the boat, he pointed to two white lights way in the distance. "See those lights?" he said. "You have to look for them. If at any point I lose my bearings, I look ahead, find the two white lights, and line them up with the front of the boat. They keep me safely going in the right direction."

Delighting in God's Wisdom

And so it is with God's wisdom. He's like the white lights in the distance. His wisdom is always there, and He is trustworthy. Let's apply what we have learned.

1. Proverbs 3:5 says, "Trust in the Lord with all your heart and lean not on your own understanding." List the areas of your life where you think you are trusting God. Are there areas of your life where you don't trust God? Can you identify these areas?

    a. In the areas where you are not trusting God, are you leaning on your own understanding? If so, explain how. Do you think you have control over these areas? What did you learn about God today that you can apply to these areas of your life?

    b. Jeremiah 17:9 tells us that "the heart is deceitful above all things and desperately wicked." With this truth in mind, how is it a trap of Satan when we trust in our own understanding?

2. Proverbs 3:6 says, "In all your ways acknowledge Him, and He shall direct your paths." We learned that acknowledging God is the same as knowing Him deeply. When we know the captain of a ship, it is easy to trust that he is navigating and leading the boat to safety. What area of your life needs God's direction or seems to be winding in a crooked direction? Write those below. Next to each area, acknowledge God's authority over it and commit each crooked path to Him.

3. Proverbs 3:23 says, "When you lie down, you will not be afraid; yes, you will lie down and your sleep will be sweet." It is often at night when the house is quiet and the room is dark that fear and anxiety keep us awake. Do you struggle with this? Proverbs 3:23 tells us we do not need to be afraid. From what you've learned, how can you trust God's protection?

   a. If nighttime is a difficult time for you, pray before you go to bed; take each care and cast it to God as we are told to do in 1 Peter 5:7. Don't take the cares and anxieties back. Leave them in God's hand. Ask God to give you sweet sleep each night.

 **DELIGHTING** in God's Word

Reflecting back on our chapter, how has the Lord prompted you to pray?

Write a verse from the chapter that God has spoken to your heart.

Close in Prayer

"The one thing I ask of the Lord - the thing I seek most - is to live in the house of the Lord all the days of my life, delighting in the Lord's perfections and meditating in his temple." Psalm 27:4

WEEK 4
STAY ON WISDOM'S PATH
Proverbs 4

The Israelite community was growing so rapidly that my work as a midwife never seemed to end. Despite our horrific living conditions and forced hard labor, God continued to bless us with more and more children. Life was lived with little comfort or pleasure but, despite it all, our numbers continued to increase.

The new king ruling over Egypt was clearly not concerned about us because the more we grew, the harsher we were treated. One day the king approached me and my fellow midwives, Puah and Shiphrah, because he knew we helped the Hebrew women when they gave birth. When he spoke with us, he commanded us to do something incomprehensible! He said to us, "When you do the duties of a midwife for the Hebrew women and see them on the birth stools, if it is a son, then you shall kill him; but if it is a daughter, then she shall live." How could we possibly obey his wicked plan? We were trained to help bring new life into the world, not kill the very children we were sent to help! More importantly, we feared God and we knew this act was sinful in His sight. What could we do? We recognized we had been given two options, and we would need to decide which one we would choose. One option led to death, the other led to life. We chose life.

It was not easy to stay the course we picked, even with our strong convictions. Nevertheless, we feared God more than we feared the king, so we chose not to kill the Hebrew baby boys. However, we knew one day the king would call for us again, and we would have to explain the continued growth of the male population. That day came last week. When we entered the king's presence, he was not happy at all! He said, "Why have you done this thing, and saved the male children?" Puah and Shiphrah did not tell him the full truth. Instead, they explained that the Hebrew women were not like the Egyptian women; for they often gave birth quickly before we arrived. This answer seemed to anger the king even more! As a result, I suspect it will not be long before he tries to put another evil plan into place to reduce the number of Hebrew boys. We made our choice to disobey the king, but we have watched God bless our lives because of our commitment to obey Him. He has established us in households, and we know this is a gift from Him as a direct response to our convictions to follow Him. (Exodus 1)

As we open Proverbs 4, you may notice Solomon's instruction is similar to things we have already studied. We know in scripture, when something is repeated we need to pay attention. Once again, Solomon warns his son to stay on the "path of the just" which is where the righteous walk, and to avoid the path of the wicked. Just as Shiphrah and Puah made a conscious decision to walk the upright road, we, too, must look for and pursue this path even when it is not the popular or easy choice. There are many blessings which accompany godliness, and we will be rewarded despite the challenges we may encounter. May we be encouraged to not only find the path but to stay steadfastly upon it, knowing it leads to life.

RECEIVING God's Word

Open in Prayer
Read Proverbs 4

EXPERIENCING God's Word

Experience 1: The Path of Wisdom - Proverbs 4:1-13

1. As Proverbs 4 begins, you will notice that once more we see Solomon speak as a father. However, this time he says, "Hear, my children" instead of "Hear, my son." We can conclude from this change that the admonitions are more general and generational in nature. Read Proverbs 4:1-2. What are the three things the father tells his children to remember?

2. Godly instruction in the home is a command by God. Read Deuteronomy 6:4-9. In these verses, what is the command to parents?

    a. In Proverbs 4:1 Solomon says to "hear his instruction." How does the instruction of a father leave an impression upon a child? Why is this so important?

3. Read Proverbs 4:3. This verse speaks about Solomon's mother and father. In order to learn more about Solomon's parents and his birth, read 2 Samuel 12:15-25. Describe the family condition leading up to his birth. What observations can you make?

4. Read Proverbs 4:4-13. The content contained in these verses may look similar to other chapters we have studied but, upon closer inspection, you will notice some differences. Answer the questions below:

    a. What do you notice about Solomon's passionate pleas?

    b. What words are used by Solomon to denote the staying power of wisdom?

    c. What does Solomon say about staying on wisdom's path?

    d. In Proverbs 4:7 Solomon says that "wisdom is the principal thing." Why should wisdom be the principal thing in our lives? Keep in mind that the word "principal" is translated as "the beginning." It is the same word used in Proverbs 1:7, but here it means "first in importance."

    e. In Proverbs 4:13 Solomon tells us "that we need to keep wisdom, for it is our life." The word life is "chay" (H2416). It comes from the word "chayah," (H2421) which can be found in verse 4b. This word speaks to being alive, the quality of life, and making known or showing this life to others. Think about this conversation for a moment. What does this say about the importance of wisdom and how we tend to it on a daily basis?

Experience 2: Two Paths - Proverbs 4:14-19

1. Read Proverbs 4:14-19. Notice there are two paths described. What are they and how are they portrayed?

a. David's last words are recorded in 2 Samuel 23:2-4. Obviously, Solomon's father's words made an impression on him. Read this passage and note the similarities between this text and Proverbs 4:14-19.

Experience 3: Ponder the Path - Proverbs 4:20-27

1. In Proverbs 4:20-27 Solomon uses references to members of our body. Read these verses and describe how each body part functions regarding wisdom and staying its course.

   - Ear

   - Eyes

   - Heart

   - Mouth

   - Foot

2. Read Romans 6:12-13. What do these verses say about how our body is to be yielded to God?

3. Read Proverbs 4:27. Here Solomon speaks of our focus to stay on the path of wisdom. What does he say can be a distraction?

   a. God repeats his command to stay the course multiple times in scripture. Read Deuteronomy 5:32-33, Deuteronomy 28:14 and Joshua 23:6. How do these verses add to what Solomon is teaching in Proverbs?

   b. Read Isaiah 30:19-21. When we get distracted, how does this verse encourage you about staying the course?

Experience 4: Shiphrah and Puah
Read Exodus 1

1. Read Exodus 1:1-10. The Jewish descendants of Jacob lived in Egypt. A new king rose up who did not know Joseph who had served as second in command to Pharaoh for many years prior. Why were the children of Israel a threat to the new king? What was he afraid of?

2. From verses 11-14 list all the ways the king tried to exert control over the Jewish people. Was it successful? Explain.

3. Read Exodus 1:15-17. The king of Egypt went to two Hebrew midwives named Shiphrah and Puah. What did he tell them to do? Why did the midwives disobey the king?

4. In Exodus 1:18-22 the king of Egypt learns that Shiphrah and Puah are not following his orders. Read these verses. How does their response to the king demonstrate they are following God's wisdom instead?

   a. How did God bless their obedience to Him?

ACTING on God's Word

About ten years ago, I (Stacy) had a dream that was so impressionable that it has stayed with me. I don't remember my dreams very often, but this one was different. I recall waking up and vividly remembering details even to this day. I don't often give dreams much weight, but I just couldn't get this one out of my head. All day long I replayed it in my mind. I brought it before the Lord in prayer, as I thought there might be a message in it for me. I believe there was.

My dream began with two very different paths before me. The path to my right was a long stretch of gravel road. The road was flat and unencumbered. But it was empty. No one else was traveling that road. To the left was a deep creek. The water was moving with the current. Sticking out of the water were large boulders scattered throughout the creek. On the boulders were people trying to navigate their way through the creek. It wasn't an easy path, but a hand was reaching out to help them. The people were struggling a bit and moving slowly. I remember looking at them and thinking, "Why are they taking that route? It looks so hard. I'm not going that way." And with that, I made my decision and started running as fast as I could down the gravel road. But I heard something behind me and looked over my shoulder. I saw a massive snake slithering down the road after me with its mouth open and, before I could take another step, its fangs grabbed ahold of my ankle. Then I woke up out of breath.

I know my tendency. I often just want to get where I'm going with the least amount of resistance. I don't want to rely on others. I have to be careful because my independence sometimes keeps me from fully depending on God. My dream, in many ways, reflected my attitude in life of self-sufficiency. I had chosen the wrong path. God made that clear. He wanted me to stay on His path and allow Him to help me along the way. As we saw in our chapter, Solomon is once again guiding his children along wisdom's path. Let's apply what we learned about staying steadfastly on this path.

1. Proverbs 4:11 says, "I have taught you in the way of wisdom; I have led you in right paths." Solomon was encouraging his children in wisdom. He had taught them and led them. We are blessed if wisdom is taught to us by our parents, but this isn't the case for everyone. If this is the case for you, what did your parents teach you regarding wisdom and God? If not, who has been influential in your life regarding wisdom?

   a. I encourage you to write a letter of thanks to either your parents or someone who has influenced your life regarding wisdom. This could be a text, a card or an email.

   b. If you are a parent, grandparent, or spiritual parent, consider those God has allowed in your sphere of influence. What do they need to be taught regarding the path of Godly wisdom? How can you go about teaching them?

2. Proverbs 4:23 says, "Keep your heart with all diligence, for out of it spring the issues of life." What do you do to diligently keep your heart set on God's wisdom?

3. Proverbs 4:26-27a says, "Ponder the path of your feet. And let all your ways be established. Do not turn to the right or the left." When was the last time you considered the destination of your present path? Why is pondering your path important?

   a. In order for our ways to be established, we need to be purposeful. Satan's greatest deterrent is distraction. Consider the ways you have been distracted from following God and seeking His wisdom. What can you do to be more purposeful, so your path is established?

4. If you had to share with someone three main truths about wisdom and God's path that have impacted your life the most, what would you share? Write them below.

D DELIGHTING in God's Word

Reflecting back on our chapter, how has the Lord prompted you to pray?

Write a verse from the chapter that God has spoken to your heart.

Close in Prayer

WEEK 5
THE IMMORAL WOMAN
Proverbs 5 & 7

She couldn't help but take notice of him. At least that's what she told herself. She was married to Potiphar, a man highly esteemed as Pharaoh's officer and the Captain of the guard. Ever since Potiphar brought Joseph into their house and gave him authority over the household, things were different. They were experiencing personal prosperity and blessing unlike ever before. Yet, she felt alone and was discontent with her life and relationship with her husband. Potiphar was consumed with his position and she seemed invisible to him. To make things worse, Joseph didn't even seem to notice her either. With each passing day, her heart longed for Joseph even more. There was something different about him. Something so alluring. Not only was he strong and handsome, but he also had a kind heart. Her thoughts were daily swept away with fantasies of him and his affection. The more she thought of him, the more she wanted him. She tried everything she could think of to get his attention. Fueled with determination, she provocatively and aggressively made her move toward him by trying to seduce him with her words and desirous appeals. Being a God-honoring man, Joseph refused her advances. He knew there was a line drawn by God and Potiphar that should never be crossed by the two of them. She was a married woman, and Potiphar's wife was not to be his.

As persistent as she was, Joseph continually said no to her advances. This angered her all the more. It wasn't long before she found herself alone with him again. All the other servants of the house were outside. Now was her chance. As he came into the house, she grabbed hold of his robe and invited him to go into the bedroom with her. Leaving his robe in her hands, Joseph abruptly pulled away from her and quickly ran out the door. She had him trapped. How dare he deny her. Embittered, angered and rejected, she knew how to get even with him. She immediately called for the men of the house to tell them that Joseph had tried to rape her. When her husband arrived home, she told him the same story. She would have the last word. In his anger, he had Joseph removed from the house and thrown into prison. (Genesis 39)

The immoral woman is at the heart of our study this week. Like Potiphar's wife, she is a woman who desires to fulfill selfish, sexual, and emotional desires outside of the marriage relationship that God has ordained. Whether that would be engaging with a married man, or a married woman desiring another man, it is immoral and sin. Proverbs 5 gives a clear warning concerning this woman. Her seductive ways can be alluring, but it will always lead to collateral destruction. Solomon warns us to not be this woman, and advises his son to avoid her at all costs. He speaks from experience. Instead of being satisfied by the wife God gave him, Solomon chose to give in to the temptation of the immoral woman. It left him, as he says, "on the verge of total ruin" (Proverbs 5:14).

Even though this is the writing of a father to his son, there is much we can apply to our lives from Solomon's admonition. In the age of digital technology, the temptation to be caught up in an emotional or physical relationship with someone who is not our husband or with someone who is married to another woman is continually present. When we feel like our needs are not being met, we are at risk of becoming the immoral woman. May we learn from Joseph's example. The secret of triumph in this area lies in our love for God and a heart that fears Him. God was with Joseph, but Joseph was also walking with God. He knew sinning in this area would be a sin before God. When temptation came, he ran for the door! May we do the same as we guard our marriages, put boundaries on opposite sex relationships and, above all, keep our hearts clinging to Jesus!

RECEIVING God's Word

Open in Prayer

Read Proverbs 5 and Proverbs 7

EXPERIENCING God's Word

Experience 1: The Immoral Woman Described - Proverbs 5:1-6 & Proverbs 7

1. Read Proverbs 5:1-2. Before Solomon gives his description of an immoral woman, he repeats four instructions to his son that will help to guard against a destructive choice. Fill in the blanks below from verses 1-2.

   "Pay attention to my _____"

   "lend your ear to my _____"

   "That you may _____ _____"

   "And your lips may keep _____."

Delighting in God's Wisdom

2. Proverbs 7 reiterates the same message regarding the immoral woman. Solomon gives his son advice, once again, regarding this woman and how to avoid her. Read Proverbs 7:1-5. Fill in the blanks below from these verses.

   "Keep my _____ and live"
   "Bind them _____ _____ _____."
   "Write them _____ _____ _____ _____ _____ _____."
   "Say to wisdom, '_____ _____ _____ _____'."
   "That they may _____ _____ from the immoral woman."

3. Proverbs 5:3 describes the comparison Solomon makes about the lips of an immoral woman to honey and oil. What does this say about the alluring power behind her words?

4. Read Proverbs 5:4a. The analogy of oil and honey is what the immoral woman uses to entice a man, but Solomon says it is a façade. What does he say is found behind the oil and honey? Explain this deception.

"Wormwood oil contains the chemical thujone which excites the central nervous system. However, it can also cause seizures and other adverse effects. Other chemicals in wormwood might decrease inflammation (swelling)." www.webmd.com/vitamins/ai/ingredientmono-729/wormwood

5. Another analogy is given regarding the ways of an immoral woman in verse 4b. How are her words described?

   a. Compare Hebrews 4:12 with Proverbs 5:4b. What do you learn about the power of her words based on this comparison?

6. What does Proverbs 5:5 say about the path of the immoral woman?

7. Read Proverb 5:6a. We are told to ponder her path. In Proverbs 4:26 Solomon told his son to ponder his own path. Explain why it is vitally important to consider both paths.

8. Read Proverbs 7:6-9. Describe the scenario Solomon witnessed of the young man who took the path to the immoral woman. What do you notice?

9. How else are the ways of an immoral woman described in Proverbs 5:6b?

10. Read Proverbs 7:10-27. What other details are given regarding the ways of the immoral woman?

Experience 2: Her Devastating Effects - Proverbs 5:7-14

1. If you recall from your study of Proverbs 1, Solomon had a major problem with infidelity. It would be his downfall. 1 Kings 11:3 tells us he had 700 wives, princesses, and 300 concubines. Clearly, he has some life experience regarding the effects of marital infidelity, and he speaks from this place. Read Proverbs 5:7-8. There is urgency in his wording, and his instruction is very simple. What is it? What does this say about sin and how it begins?

2. Read Proverbs 5:9-11. How will an immoral choice affect:

   a. Your reputation:

   b. Your future:

   c. Your possessions:

   d. Your physical body:

3. In verses 12-14, Solomon describes the posture of the heart of someone who chose to enter into an adulterous relationship. What did he do with the Biblical instruction he had received?

   a. Do you hear any remorse in his words in these verses? Explain.

   b. Looking at verse 14, how did this decision impact his social and professional relationships?

4. Read Malachi 3:5. What is God's heart toward the adulterer and why?

Experience 3: Pure Pleasure: God's Design - Proverbs 5:15-23

1. Read Proverbs 5:15-17. Solomon compares sexual intimacy with drinking water from your own cistern. How does he caution his son about keeping the water pure?

2. In Proverbs 5:18-19 we see the beautiful satisfaction that can be enjoyed when sexual intimacy is fulfilled according to God's design. How is it described in these verses?

3. Look up the following verses about God's design for intimacy in a married relationship with one man and one woman. Note below what you learn.

    a. Genesis 1:27-28

    b. Genesis 2:22-25

    c. Malachi 2:14-15

    d. 1 Corinthians 7:1-3

    e. Hebrews 13:4

4. Read Proverbs 5:20. Solomon asks a rhetorical question. What is it?

5. The eyes of the Lord are described in verses 21-23. How does this demonstrate why what might be considered "secret" is never truly hidden?

   a. What does verse 22 say about our choice in making wise decisions?

   b. We need to call sin, sin. One of the greatest problems of our culture today is that we fail to do so and we give excuses for our choices. Fill in the blank below:

   Intimacy outside of the marriage relationship between a man and a woman is _____.

   c. We are given a very stern warning in Proverbs 5:23. What is the end result for the person who chooses to enter into adultery?

Experience 4: Potiphar's Wife
Read Genesis 39

1. Read Genesis 39:1-7. How is Joseph described? What effect does he have on Potiphar's wife?

2. Read verses 7-23. What does Potiphar's wife do to Joseph?

3. Describe how Potiphar's wife fills the description of the immoral woman in Proverbs 5 & 7.

ACTING on God's Word

Whether you are single or married, the command from the Lord is the same; do not commit adultery (Exodus 20:14). For the single woman that means not getting involved with someone who is already married. For the married woman that means safeguarding, strengthening and tending to your marriage so you do not fall into temptation or commit adultery. I (Brenda) have divided up the acting portion into two categories based upon your marital status. Please choose from one of the two groups on the following page and answer the following questions.

For the Single Woman:

Being single can certainly be a fun and exciting time in a woman's life. There are freedoms available to a single woman that a married woman can no longer enjoy. However, if you are single and dating, God has instructed that there is one person who is unavailable to you and that is a married man. God's Word is very clear on this topic, and His instructions are not only for your benefit, but also for the man's. The married man has made a commitment to someone else which is a covenant before God and to his wife for the rest of his life. If you choose to get involved with him, you are messing with God's plan for his life. That alone should stop you in your tracks. Furthermore, if you get involved with him, you will be destroying his home. His wife is counting on him to keep his commitment and so are his children, if he has any. I have seen many marriages destroyed by adultery, and I can honestly say I have never seen good results come from an adulterous relationship. I strongly urge you to completely avoid dating or being involved with anyone who is married!

1. List several phrases Solomon used to describe an adulterous woman from Proverbs 5.

2. Reread the phrases you just wrote. How would you be the very woman described above if you got involved with a married man?

3. Describe what you consider to be an emotional affair.

   a. Why can an emotional affair be just as damaging as a physical affair? Why should it be avoided?

4. Describe what you consider to be flirting.

   a. How can flirting with a married man lead to an adulterous relationship? Why should you avoid it?

Close your time out today in prayer. Confess any actions or thoughts that are adulterous. If you are looking to be married, ask the Lord to make you content as you wait for Him to provide a God-fearing, single man who will be faithful to you until death do you part.

For the Married Woman:

I have been married for nearly 25 years to my husband, Mike, and despite our marital status, over the years we both have encountered people who have expressed interest in pursuing a relationship with us. I praise God for His safekeeping of our marriage, both physically and emotionally. But I will tell you it has required a serious commitment to the Lord, dedication to each other, being resolute in our decision making, and exhibiting self-control. In a world where the morality plumb line seems to have plummeted to an all-time low, and where pornography, swinging and divorce are rampant, Mike and I have made the conscious decision to keep our marriage vows. I alone am Mike's, and he alone is mine. What about you?

1. What did you promise to your husband as you stood before God on your wedding day? Write as many vows as you can remember.

    a. If possible, get a written copy of your wedding vows and re-read them or, if it was recorded, listen to or watch your wedding ceremony. What did you promise your husband that day? How are you doing on fulfilling your promises on a daily basis?

Delighting in God's Wisdom

2. In the area of marital faithfulness, describe your steadfast commitment to your husband.

   a. Is there someone in your life that has the potential to compromise your promise to your husband, either physically or emotionally? If so, what is your plan to safeguard your marriage from him or, sadly in our culture, her?

   b. Has bitterness or unforgiveness toward your husband become a problem? Is it keeping you from enjoying all the promises you made or from deep intimacy with him? How will you seek reconciliation in this area?

3. Describe why praying together as a married couple is one of the most important things we can do for one another. How are you putting this into practice?

a. Describe how spending time with other God-fearing, happily married couples can strengthen your marriage.

4. If you have children, why is honoring your marriage vows vitally important for the future of your children? What message does a strong marriage communicate to your children?

5. What did you learn from Proverbs chapters 5 & 7 about the adulterous woman that stood out to you? Why are her actions to be avoided at all costs?

Close your time out in prayer. Confess any actions or thoughts that are adulterous. Ask the Lord to give you deep contentment in the husband of your youth and to keep you from any form of adultery.

 D DELIGHTING in God's Word

Reflecting back on our chapters, how has the Lord prompted you to pray?

Write a verse that God has spoken to your heart.

Close in Prayer

"The one thing I ask of the Lord - the thing I seek most - is to live in the house of the Lord all the days of my life, delighting in the Lord's perfections and meditating in his temple." Psalm 27:4

WEEK 6
BE AWARE OF FOOLISHNESS

Proverbs 6

She was a God-fearing, wise woman known for her tenderness and striking beauty. Her outward appearance reflected the beauty that came from her heart, despite the heartache that plagued her day in and day out. She was married to a ruthless, power hungry and prideful man who was known through the Judean region as a man of great wealth. Yet all the money in the world held little value compared to her desire to be treated kindly by her husband. He only looked out for himself and nothing could stop him from getting what he wanted. Everything he did dripped of evil intent. Nabal, meaning fool, was his name. His very name defined his character. He declared to everyone that he was a fool, and his behaviors proved it. But through it all, Abigail remained faithful and steadfast.

One afternoon Abigail was approached by one of Nabal's young men who told her some very distressing news about how her husband had treated David. Known throughout the area as a great soldier, David was highly respected by all. The young man explained to Abigail that David's army both protected them and their sheep from the Philistines. At shearing time David kindly asked for Nabal to return the favor by giving supplies to him and his men. Nabal foolishly replied with insults and critical words about David. Angry, David planned to bring retribution against Nabal and his entire household.

Abigail knew she had to act quickly to protect her home and her foolish husband. Time was of the essence. Knowing her husband's evil character, Abigail wisely kept her plan quiet. She loaded donkeys with bread, fruit, meat, and wine and sent her servants ahead of her to meet David. Under the cover of the hillside, she came to David. In humble submission and great reverence, she bowed before him. Pleading for forgiveness, she asked that Nabal's foolishness be put on her. Then with boldness and great courage, she reminded David that God would avenge him and deal with Nabal. She also reminded him that his future was secure as God had appointed him ruler over Israel. David praised Abigail for her Godly wisdom. (1 Samuel 25)

Every day we encounter Nabals and Abigails. Every day we are faced with our own responses and choices regarding our behavior. Will we act like Abigail by responding to foolish behavior with wisdom and discernment, or will we act like Nabal by elevating our wants and desires above everyone else's? In Proverbs 6 we will be introduced to four different types of foolish people. These are not first-time introductions. I imagine we can see their foolish behaviors mirrored in ourselves or others. Solomon will instruct us to watch out for the imposter, the lazy person, the wicked person and the adulterous person.

Delighting in God's Wisdom

He will warn us of their foolishness and will speak plainly of the consequences for falling into their evil traps. He will also tell us of the seven sins that are detestable to God. The answers will always be found in God's wisdom when dealing with foolish behaviors and the sins of the heart. Wisdom not only guards us but also protects us, and, like Abigail, fuels our wise and diligent response in the face of evil. May Abigail be our example and God's Word be our instruction so that we may live a life pleasing to God; saying no to foolishness and yes to His wisdom.

RECEIVING God's Word

Open in Prayer
Read Proverbs 6

EXPERIENCING God's Word

Experience 1: The Imposing Person - Proverbs 6:1-5

1. Read Proverbs 6:1-2. What warning does Solomon give to his son? Our agreement with this foolish request can entrap us. Explain.

2. In verses 3-4 Solomon's son is encouraged to save himself from the trap of the imposing person. Read the following phrases taken from these verses and write the deliverance instructions in your own words below.

"Go"

"humble yourself"

"plead with your friend"

"give no sleep to your eyes"

3. Read Proverbs 3:5. Two comparisons have been made between the imposer and the wise person. Explain the comparisons.

Experience 2: The Lazy Person - Proverbs 6:6-11

1. In Proverbs 6:6-8 Solomon gives us an object lesson in nature concerning the wise person and the lazy person. What does he use for the object lesson? Explain the comparison.

"Solomon's interest in the ant centered on the colony's work ethic and on the fact that ants do not have to be forced to work. Ants are not slothful. They are an example of industry. They do not need slave drivers to make sure they get up in the morning and fulfill their appointed tasks. Let the slothful man consider that! The ant works without force." (John Phillips, *The John Phillips Commentary Series: Exploring Proverbs Volume One*, p.138-139.)

2. Read Proverbs 6:9. What does the sluggard do with his time and why is it equated with laziness?

3. God has a lot to say about laziness. Read the following verses and note what you learn.

   Proverbs 12:24

   Proverbs 15:19

   Proverbs 26:14-15

4. Read Proverbs 6:10-11. What is the motto of the lazy person? What is the outcome of lazy behavior?

Experience 3: The Evil Person - Proverbs 6:12-19

1. Read Proverbs 6:12-15 and answer the questions below.

   a.   What comes out of his mouth? (v.12)

   b.   How do his eyes communicate his motives? (v. 13)

   c.   How does he walk? (v.12-13)

    d. What do his fingers do and what does this mean? (v.13)

    e. What is in his heart? (v.14)

    f. What is the result of his actions to those around him? (v. 14-15)

2. Go back to verse 12. The evil person is called "worthless." In the KJV he is called "naughty." This word is "beliya'al" (H1100) in Hebrew. It means to be "unprofitable, wicked or good for nothing." Is the person or their behavior worthless? Explain.

3. In verse 15 the judgment of the foolish, evil person is described. It says, "He shall be broken without remedy." Read Isaiah 30:12-15 and answer the following questions.

    a. What does a foolish person do that causes judgment to come to him?

    b. From these verses, describe God's judgment.

   c. In verse 15 the remedy is given. What is it and what action is required of the evil person?

4. Read Proverbs 6:16-19. In these verses the actions of the evil man are given a name. They are hated by God and called abominations. Notice in verses 16-19 that the same parts of the body were used in verses 12-15. Look at the body parts below and list the sin(s) that are ascribed to each part according to verses 16-19.

   - Eyes

   - Tongue/Mouth

   - Hands

   - Heart

   - Feet

5. God tells us in Proverbs 6:16-19 that there are sins that are an abomination to Him. How are the things God hates opposite of who He is fundamentally? Finish the sentences below.

   God hates a proud look because God is…

   God hates a lying tongue because God is…

   God hates hands that shed innocent blood because God is…

   God hates a heart that devises wicked plans because God is…

God hates feet that are swift in running to evil because God is…

God hates a false witness who speaks lies because God is…

God hates one who sows discord among the brethren because God is…

Experience 4: The Adulterous Person - Proverbs 6:20-35

1. Read Proverbs 6:20-23 and Deuteronomy 6:6-9. Deuteronomy 6:6-9 is God's command to parents regarding how to train up their children. Solomon would have known Deuteronomy 6:6-9. What similarities do you see in these two sets of verses?

   a. Read Proverbs 6:24. From what you just learned in the previous three verses, how does the influence of the Word of God protect the wise from the foolish?

2. Read Proverbs 6:25-29. What are the consequences of falling for the foolish behavior of the seductress or any foolishness that seduces us?

Delighting in God's Wisdom

> "Again, we are reminded that it is the heart which must be kept or guarded if the feet would be preserved from forbidden paths. Sorrow and poverty – spiritual and natural – will be the dread result if there is any tampering with uncleanness." (*Notes on the Book of Proverbs*, H.A. Ironside, pg. 17)

3. Read Proverbs 6:30-31. Here we find the description of a thief who is stealing because he is starving. In Exodus 22:1-4 God lays out restitution for the thief who is caught. What is the restitution available for the thief in Proverbs 6:30-31?

4. In Proverbs 6:32-35, a description is given of the judgment brought against an adulterer. What is the restitution for the person who commits adultery? Explain.

Experience 5: Abigail
Read 1 Samuel 25

1. Read 1 Samuel 25:1-3. How is Nabal described? How is Abigail described?

2. David, who had just been named as King Saul's successor, is in the wilderness of Paran near Carmel. Nabal's servants are shearing sheep in Carmel. David sends ten young men to the wilderness when he hears that Nabal's servants are there shearing Nabal's sheep. Read 1 Samuel 25:14-16 and explain how David's servants helped Nabal.

3. Go back in the chapter to verse 4 and let's pick up there. Read 1 Samuel 25:4-13. David sends his ten servants to Nabal to ask for repayment for helping protect his men and sheep. David knows it is shearing time, which is a time of great wealth, so Nabal will have more than enough provisions from which to give. How does Nabal respond?

   a. Why does David respond with such anger? Read verses 21-22 to get a deeper look into his anger toward Nabal.

4. One of the young men tells Nabal's wife, Abigail, what has happened. Read verses 14-44 and explain her wise actions and how those actions are received by others.

Delighting in God's Wisdom

a. How does God bless her for acting wisely?

A ACTING on God's Word

While growing up, my dad often would say to me (Brenda), "Obey me now, and you can thank me later." Interestingly, as an adult, I am thankful for the times I obeyed my parents because their counsel and Godly instruction kept me from destructive behaviors. They taught me to avoid certain things because they loved me and did not want me to be harmed. It is similar with God. He hates certain things and wants us to avoid them because of His great love for us.

In Proverbs 6 there are four foolish people Solomon tells his son to avoid. They are the imposing person, the lazy person, the evil person and the adulterous person. Below you will find a few scenarios that could result when encountering these individuals. Read the descriptions below and write the Biblical counsel you would give in response to the situation.

<u>The Imposer:</u>

"A friend has asked me to co-sign their loan for a new car. They are presently unemployed but say they are about to be hired by a large, successful company. They need the car to get to this job. They say I'll get my money back each month in installments. What should I do?"

Your Biblical Response from Proverbs 6:1-5:

The Lazy Person:

"My child is neither working this summer nor participating in any other extra-curricular activities. He sleeps late, doesn't pick up after himself, and spends too much time on his phone and in front of screens. What should I do?"

Your Biblical Response from Proverbs 6:6-11:

The Evil Person:

"Seems like any time I get into a conversation with my next-door neighbor, she always talks negatively about the other neighbors. She is quick to point out all of their flaws while making herself seem as though she is perfect. She speaks poorly about their marriages, their decisions and their parenting choices. She is always villainizing them and assigning evil intent to their actions. I know some of these same neighbors and do not observe the same things. Every conversation with her is divisive. What should I do?"

Your Biblical Response from Proverbs 6:12-19:

The Adulterous Person:

"I have an old high school friend who reached out to me through social media, and she shared that her marriage is struggling. She thinks her husband is having an affair. She would like to connect with me and some of our other high school friends in Las Vegas for a girls' weekend. I am not busy that weekend and she invited me to join her. She detailed the plans for the weekend which include drinking, attending a risqué show, and hopefully having a 'no strings attached' weekend. It seems her intent is to show her husband that she can have a good time too. What should I do?"

Your Biblical Response from Proverbs 6:20-35:

1. Which type of foolish behavior characterized above snares you most often and why?

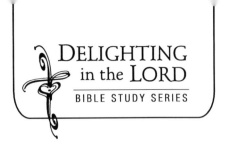

2. When we engage in foolish behaviors, we don't always consider the consequences before acting. What did you learn today about foolish behaviors and their consequences that enables you to act wisely the next time you encounter these four types of people?

DELIGHTING in God's Word

Reflecting back on our chapter, how has the Lord prompted you to pray?

Write a verse from the chapter that God has spoken to your heart.

Close in Prayer

"The one thing I ask of the Lord - the thing I seek most - is to live in the house of the Lord all the days of my life, delighting in the Lord's perfections and meditating in his temple." Psalm 27:4

WEEK 7

WISDOM'S INVITATION

Proverbs 8

Evening was falling over the land of Jericho when two strangers approached Rahab, the prostitute, at her home. One could imagine these men were different than the others who came to Rahab. They were Israelites. When they requested lodging for the night, it was made very clear they were not looking for a sexual encounter, but rather shelter. It certainly seems this was not Rahab's typical customer; however, she escorted them into her home and listened as they explained their situation further. They told Rahab they were Israelite spies who had come to examine the city and needed a safe place to stay until they could slip back out of town without being noticed. No sooner had Rahab agreed to allow them to stay with her, when a knock came at her door. It was men with a message from the king of Jericho saying, "Bring out the men who have come to you, who have entered your house, for they have come to search out all the country." (Joshua 2:3) Before answering the door, she hurried the men up to her roof and told them to hide under the flax she had spread out on her rooftop. Rahab needed to think fast. When she answered the door, she told the king's messengers that indeed two men had visited her, but she did not know where they were from or where they were going. However, she did see them leave the city gates at dark. She encouraged the messengers to pursue the men toward the Jordan and convinced them that, if they acted quickly, surely they would catch up to the men.

Once the king's messengers were gone, Rahab went up to the roof to talk with the Israelites. She had heard plenty about how the Israelites' God had rescued them and wanted to know more about the One they called the Living God. She may have been only a prostitute to everyone in Jericho, but she was wise enough to see an opportunity when it presented itself. She approached the two spies and said, "I know that the LORD has given you the land, that the terror of you has fallen on us, and that all the inhabitants of the land are fainthearted because of you. For we have heard how the LORD dried up the water of the Red Sea for you when you came out of Egypt, and what you did to the two kings of the Amorites who were on the other side of the Jordan, Sihon and Og, whom you utterly destroyed. And as soon as we heard these things, our hearts melted; neither did there remain any more courage in anyone because of you, for the LORD your God, He is God in heaven above and on earth beneath. Now therefore, I beg you, swear to me by the LORD, since I have shown you kindness, that you also will show kindness to my father's house, and give me a true token, and spare my father, my mother, my brothers, my sisters, and all that they have, and deliver our lives from death." (Joshua 2:9-13)

The spies agreed to Rahab's request, with the understanding that she would keep their business a secret and get them safely out of the city. Then, when they return to overtake Jericho, she would have a scarlet cord bound to her window where they could see it, and all of her family would have to be inside her house with her. Their agreement was reached, and both parties would be safe. Rahab encouraged the men to escape to the mountains by using a rope through her window. Because Rahab's house was situated on the city wall, the men escaped into the night without being noticed.

As we study Proverbs 8, we will notice that wisdom is like an invitation that must be accepted. It will cry out to the receiver, but it must be recognizable and desired by the recipient or it will fall on deaf ears. We will learn that God's wisdom has been available since the beginning of time, and, when it is embraced, it is accompanied by many blessings.

Rahab recognized that the wisdom she desired about God was delivered to her door by way of two spies. She believed that the stories about the God of Israel were true. So when the men from that country stood before her, she seized the opportunity to learn more. She believed God was ruling over heaven and the earth below, and she trusted in Him. Through Rahab's faith, she gained her salvation as well as many other blessings to come through the men whose God was the LORD.

We may hear wisdom's invitation calling to us too. Are we listening? Do we know what it sounds like? Are we willing and humble recipients? Do we acknowledge that God has held all wisdom in Him since the beginning of time? Will we reach out and open the invitation, or will we reject it in favor of our own human understanding?

RECEIVING God's Word

Open in Prayer
Read Proverbs 8

 E EXPERIENCING God's Word

Experience 1: Wisdom Cries Out - Proverbs 8:1-11

1. Read Proverbs 8:1-3. Wisdom is once again personified as a woman. Where is wisdom when she gives her invitation? What does her invitation sound like?

2. In verses 4 and 5, to whom is wisdom extending her invitation?

3. Read verses 6-9 and describe wisdom's speech below. How is this such a contrast when compared to how wickedness speaks?

4. In verses 10 and 11 we are told to receive wisdom's invitation because it holds value beyond the riches of this world. Explain why this is true.

Experience 2: Wisdom Sounds Like... - Proverbs 8:12-21

1. The personal pronoun being used from Proverbs 8:12-36 has now shifted from "she" to "I". Read verses 12 and 13. In order to accept wisdom's invitation, we must approach God with the correct heart attitude. What are the attitudes found in verse 13 that we should avoid?

"The abundance of personal pronouns (I, mine, me, my – 16 occurrences in 10 verses) makes wisdom herself the focus and not her rewards." (John Walvoord and Roy Zuck, *The Bible Knowledge Commentary Old Testament*, page 921)

2. Read Proverbs 8:14-21. Following is a list of wisdom's attributes that are the same as God's attributes. Keep in mind that wisdom is an attribute of God. Now, read the list of verses on the right and connect the proper verse about God with the attribute on the left.

Wisdom is...	God is...
Counselor	1 John 4:8
Understanding/wisdom	Acts 3:14
Strength	Job 9:4
Sovereign	Philippians 4:19
Love	John 14:26
Rich	1 John 3:7
Righteous	Philippians 4:13
Just	Romans 13:1

Delighting in God's Wisdom

Experience 3: Wisdom from the Beginning - Proverbs 8:22-31

1. In Proverbs 8:22 wisdom is now referred to as "me" but will return to "I" in verse 23. According to verses 22-23, when did wisdom begin and with whom?

   a. Read Genesis 1:1-2 and John 1:1-3. What do these verses tell you about wisdom's foundation?

   b. Read Romans 1:20-26. What has man done with the wisdom of God that has been clearly manifested in creation?

2. Read Proverbs 8:22-31. Wisdom is described as being possessed by God from the beginning of time. Wisdom participated with God in creation. Read the following verses that go with each day of creation taken from Genesis 1 and 2 and link wisdom's participation from Proverbs 8:22-31 with the days of creation.

Day 1 – Genesis 1:3-5:

Day 2 – Genesis 1:6-8:

Day 3 – Genesis 1:9-13:

Day 4 – Genesis 1:14-19:

Day 5 – Genesis 1:20-23:

Day 6 – Genesis 1:24-31:

Day 7 – Genesis 2:1-3:

3. From Proverbs 8:30-31, how is wisdom described in relationship to God and man?

Experience 4: Wisdom's Blessings - Proverbs 8:32-36

1. According to Proverbs 8:32-34, how does someone receive wisdom's blessings?

2. What are the blessings promised by God when someone receives His wisdom according to verse 35? Explain.

3. Read Proverbs 8:36. What does God say will happen to the person who rejects His wisdom? What is the result?

Experience 5: Rahab
Read Joshua 2

1. Read Joshua 2:1-7. Joshua sent two Israelites to secretly spy out the land of Canaan, focusing on the city of Jericho. This is the land God promised the children of Israel, going back to His promise to Abraham in Genesis 13 & 17. It is also enemy territory for the Jews. The spies came to Rahab's house. How is Rahab described and what happens when the king learns the spies are at her house?

2. From verses 8-13, put in your own words the things that she declared to the two spies concerning the LORD. How did Rahab recognize wisdom when it called through these two spies? Keep in mind too, that Rahab uses the word "LORD" which speaks of His personal name, "Yahweh."

    a. How did Rahab respond to wisdom's invitation?

3. Read verses 14-24. Explain how the LORD used these circumstances to deliver many people.

A ACTING on God's Word

Solomon was just 20 years old when he became king of Israel. Just north of Jerusalem was a place called Gibeon where Canaanite worship took place. Many went to the high places there to offer sacrifices to God as there was no temple for worship. Solomon loved God but still sacrificed and burned incense at the high places. It was here where the LORD appeared to Solomon in a dream at night early in his reign. The LORD called out to Solomon saying, "Ask! What shall I give you?" (1 Kings 3:5) Solomon recognized the voice of the LORD. Feeling young and inexperienced as well as knowing God had placed him in authority over His people, Solomon knew that he needed God's wisdom in order to rule well. He needed an understanding heart and discernment over people's motives, whether they were good or evil. The LORD was so pleased with Solomon for recognizing his need for God's wisdom that He gave Solomon riches and honor as well. The LORD told Solomon that if he heeded His wisdom and kept His commandments, that long life would come to him.

Solomon writes to us from the very things he learned and experienced. Just as he needed wisdom, so do we. The wisdom he gained he wanted to pass on. Wisdom isn't a collection of knowledge; it is having good judgment based on knowledge. It is the ability to take knowledge and discern truth so that honorable decisions are made. Solomon's example of seeking wisdom and walking in wisdom are held near to my (Stacy's) heart. God used Solomon's example in my life when He called me into Women's Ministry. My plea to God was similar, even down to the words I used in prayer telling God that I was "young and inexperienced" (1 Chronicles 29), and the responsibility was too big. I needed God's wisdom and, one morning while praying, God led me to the story of Solomon as he confirmed His calling to me through His Word.

Delighting in God's Wisdom

Life can be daunting sometimes, and God can use circumstances to show us that His wisdom is what we need. Wisdom was there in the beginning of time and remains available each day for our asking and receiving. Let's take some verses from the lesson and apply them to our lives.

1. Proverbs 8:1 says, "Does not wisdom cry out, and understanding lift up her voice?" Before Solomon cried out to the LORD for wisdom, the LORD called out to Solomon in a dream. Wisdom seeks, calls and pursues. God's wisdom does not lurk in dark corners. He proclaims His invitation to wisdom openly and frequently. His wisdom calls out to us in difficult situations. How have you seen wisdom cry out to you and understanding lift up her voice in a situation you either have gone through or are currently going through?

2. Proverbs 8:6a says, "Listen, for I will speak of excellent things, and from the opening of my lips will come right things; for my mouth will speak truth." When wisdom calls, this verse tells us that we must listen. It has been said that people are better talkers than listeners. Why is listening so important in regard to wisdom? Is listening hard for you? Explain.

    a. What simple things can you implement to help you be a better listener when it comes to hearing God speak His wisdom to you?

3. Proverbs 8:10a says, "Receive my instruction, and not silver, and knowledge rather than choice gold." Here we are told that a response is needed when wisdom calls. When we have to make choices, worldly wisdom competes with God's wisdom. Is this true for you in any area? What worldly wisdom is competing in your heart right now that is trying to be heard over God's wisdom? What is worldly wisdom saying? What is the wisdom from God saying?

4. Proverbs 8:34-35 says, "Blessed is the man who listens to me, watching daily at my gates, waiting at the posts of my doors. For whoever finds me finds life, and obtains favor from the LORD." Describe a situation in your life where wisdom brought a quality of life that only comes from God.

 DELIGHTING in God's Word

Reflecting back on our chapter, how has the Lord prompted you to pray?

Write a verse from the chapter that God has spoken to your heart.

Close in Prayer

"The one thing I ask of the Lord - the thing I seek most - is to live in the house of the Lord all the days of my life, delighting in the Lord's perfections and meditating in his temple." Psalm 27:4

WEEK 8

THE HOUSES THEY BUILT: MISS WISDOM AND MISS FOLLY

Proverbs 9

One could imagine, it was a hard life for a woman living in Philippi. Lydia knew the commercial center of Macedonia in Philippi was the best place to be practicing her trade. Tirelessly she worked, day in and day out, gathering the shellfish by the sea that held her precious purple dye. Drop by drop she collected the dye with patience and perseverance. She knew her livelihood and her family depended on it. Her wisdom and diligence paid off as many sought her out for her wares.

That Sabbath day Lydia made her way out of the city to the riverside for prayer and worship. As many gathered, she overhead a few women speaking to two men who apparently had just spent days traveling through the region. Lydia's heart was pricked as she heard them speak of God. The things they spoke of, she desired. They were speaking of Jesus, sin and salvation. She needed Jesus and received all that Paul and Silas shared. That day she and her whole household were baptized, putting their faith in Jesus. Overjoyed with gratitude towards Paul and Silas, she invited them to come stay at her home.

In Proverbs 9 we will be meeting two very different woman. We will call one Miss Wisdom and the other Miss Folly. Each woman has built a house, but their homes look very different and serve very different purposes. You will see Miss Wisdom, like Lydia, work tirelessly, intelligently and resourcefully. She will build a strong and secure home whose foundation is set on God. Her heart will be set on hospitality and invites all who desire to come. She will invite them to stay with her and share a meal in the hopes of not only filling their bellies but also their hearts with the things of God. She never left any detail overlooked, always had an open door to both the wise and the foolish, and desired to offer others a life of blessing that only comes from God.

Miss Folly, you will see, is quite the opposite. She is foolish in all she does; lazy, loud, and unskilled. Sitting idly in her doorstep day in and day out, she calls to those who pass by but offers them nothing of value. Her house is unstable, just like her ways. Both women built a house, but only one knew a strong foundation's secret; the house must stand on the knowledge of God. In God is wisdom and understanding. Lydia knew this and Miss Wisdom knew this. Do you?

 RECEIVING God's Word

Open in Prayer
Read Proverbs 9

EXPERIENCING God's Word

Experience 1: The House Wisdom Built - Proverbs 9:1-12

1. In Proverbs 9:1-3 wisdom is referred to as a woman once again. She has been busy at work building her home and preparing a banquet. Listed below are all the things that Miss Wisdom has accomplished while working and preparing. Next to each phrase, describe in your own words the importance of her work and the character trait it takes for these to be accomplished.

Verse	Importance	Character Trait Exhibited
v. 1 "hewn out her seven pillars"		
v. 2 "slaughtered her meat"		
v. 2 "mixed her wine"		
v. 2 "furnished her table"		
v. 3 "sent out her maidens"		

2. Read Proverbs 9:3-6. Answer the following questions from these verses.

   a. Miss Wisdom is not exclusive in who she invites to her home and banquet. How does she go about inviting people?

b. What three different types of people does she make sure to include? Why?

c. According to verse 6, why does Miss Wisdom eagerly extend this invitation for wisdom?

d. What do her actions convey about her heart toward others?

e. How do you see God's heart represented in her actions?

3. In Proverbs 9:7-9 Miss Wisdom addresses four different types of people: the scoffer, the wicked man, the wise man and the just man. She knows these people well and warns what might happen if they are corrected, rebuked, instructed or taught. Next to each type of person listed below, write the warned response.

- "the scoffer" (corrected)
  Warned response:

- "the wicked man" (rebuked)
  Warned response:

- "the wise man" (instructed)
  Warned response:

- "the just man" (taught)
  Warned response:

a. Read Matthew 7:6. How does this reinforce the warning Miss Wisdom gives in Proverbs 9:7-9?

4. Although stated slightly differently in Proverbs 1:7, the central theme of Proverbs is repeated again in Proverbs 9:10. Compare these two verses. How do they add to your understanding of wisdom?

   a. Wisdom and knowledge come from an understanding of God. Explain why wisdom begins with a right relationship to God.

5. Read Proverbs 9:11. What benefit does wisdom bring to life?

6. According to Proverbs 9:12, who is ultimately affected by choosing wisdom or scoffing at wisdom?

Experience 2: The House Folly Built: Proverbs 9:13-18

1. The foolish woman is described in Proverbs 9:13-18. She, too, builds a house, but her ways are much different from Miss Wisdom's building strategy. How is Miss Folly described in Proverbs 9:13? Explain these descriptions in your own words.

Delighting in God's Wisdom

2. We were told back in Proverbs 8:3 that wisdom sits in the place of prominence at the city gate, and in Proverbs 9:3 Miss Wisdom cries out from the highest places of the city. According to Proverbs 9:14, where does Miss Folly sit and how does she undermine Miss Wisdom?

3. Read Proverbs 9:15-17. Miss Folly also invites the simple and those who lack understanding. What does her invitation sound like?

   a. Does she have a banquet prepared for her guests? What does she offer them?

4. In Proverbs 9:11 we learned that Miss Wisdom offers life and blessings. According to Proverbs 9:18, what does Miss Folly offer those who accept her invitation?

5. Read Matthew 7:24-27. Describe the house of the wise and the house of the fool. How does this reinforce what was taught in Proverbs 9?

Experience 3: Lydia
Read Acts 16:6-15

1. Read Acts 16:6-14. Paul, Timothy, Silas and Luke are called by God to go to Macedonia to preach the Gospel. What do they do on the Sabbath day and who do they speak to?

2. From verse 14-15, how is Lydia described and how does she respond to Paul's message of the Gospel?

3. From verses 11-15, describe how Lydia is an example of a woman who built her house on wisdom.

ACTING on God's Word

This past summer I (Brenda) finally decided to tackle remodeling my downstairs living room, dining room and entryway. These three rooms had not been updated since we moved into the house over 20 years ago. Needless to say, the task was long overdue. I decided that I would not hire a general contractor but would oversee the project myself. As each person was hired to do the work necessary for the remodeling, delays inevitably occurred, mistakes were made, and the entire job took much longer than I had anticipated. Throughout the summer, I would look around at drop cloths, heavy layers of dust and partially completed rooms and grow weary of the lengthy process. Although I was not sorry to see my outdated hunter green carpet, floral curtains and gold fixtures taken down, I couldn't wait to see the rooms completed. One day I lamented on the phone to Stacy (who enjoys taking on such projects!) how tired I was of the upheaval in my house and how frustrated I was at how many delays I had encountered. Stacy reminded me that although the chaos of remodeling is not fun, the end result is worth all the work and disruption. Now that the project is done, I must say, I do love how the downstairs has turned out. As I look around at the fresh paint, wood floors, new carpet and updated accents, I can say it was well worth the effort.

Delighting in God's Wisdom

Miss Wisdom is also working on her house in Proverbs 9. She has not hired a general contractor nor sub-contractors. She completes much of the hard work herself. We do not read about her growing weary of the tasks nor exhibiting frustration over what she needs to complete. In fact, Proverbs reads in such a way that we could easily conclude that she is enthusiastic about her work and productivity. Perhaps Miss Wisdom is looking ahead to what the finished product will look like when it is completed rather than getting bogged down in the process. Regardless, she seems to understand that a job well done requires hard work, and she is willing to do it. Let's examine Miss Wisdom's ways and see what we can glean from her approach as well as the blessing that results.

1. Proverbs 9:1-2 says, "Wisdom has built her house, she has hewn out her seven pillars; she has slaughtered her meat, she has mixed her wine, she has also furnished her table." These are tasks that wisdom completes. How is Miss Wisdom taking care of her home?

    a. How does Miss Wisdom demonstrate Godly wisdom in her actions?

2. Proverbs 9:4a and verse 6 say this, "Whoever is simple, let him turn in here! Forsake foolishness and live, and go in the way of understanding." How is Miss Wisdom taking care of others?

    a. Why is reaching out to others after caring for our home demonstrating wisdom?

3. Proverbs 9:10 says this, "The fear of the LORD is the beginning of wisdom and the knowledge of the Holy One is understanding." How does Miss Wisdom take care of herself?

    a. Why is it important to tend to our own mind, body, soul and spirit? How does this demonstrate wisdom?

4. Proverbs 9:11 says this, "For by me your days will be multiplied, and years of your life will be added to you." How can this be a blessing to Miss Wisdom?

 **D** **DELIGHTING** in God's Word

Reflecting back on our chapter, how has the Lord prompted you to pray?

Write a verse from the chapter that God has spoken to your heart.

Close in Prayer

"The one thing I ask of the Lord - the thing I seek most - is to live in the house of the Lord all the days of my life, delighting in the Lord's perfections and meditating in his temple." Psalm 27:4

WEEK 9
FAMILY MATTERS

Selected Verses from Proverbs 10-30

"Then Isaac brought her [Rebekah] into his mother Sarah's tent; and he took Rebekah and she became his wife, and he loved her. So, Isaac was comforted after his mother's death."
(Genesis 24:67)

Her marriage to Isaac had been like a story from a fairy tale. Isaac's servant had come to her home town in search of her family and, in God's providence, she encountered him while drawing water at the well. Isaac's servant lavished her with great gifts and asked to meet her family. When they arrived home, he shared with them how he prayed for God to direct his steps to the woman his master was to marry, and she was that woman! It was a whirlwind of preparations to leave home and to travel to meet Isaac. He loved her immediately. But, those days must have seemed as if they were a million years ago as she watched her beloved son, Jacob, flee Canaan. The road she traveled to meet Isaac was now the route Jacob was using to flee to her family and away from his angry older brother, Esau. Did she have remorse over what she had done?

I (Brenda) can imagine deep regret washed over Rebekah as she thought about her decisions as a mother. She couldn't deny that she loved Jacob so much more than his twin brother, Esau, as the boys could not have been more different from one another! Jacob was so easy to love; he was so mild mannered, and he desired to be around her home. Esau was uncouth, red and hairy and loved being in the fields working. At home, he just never seemed to be content. Now, in hindsight, she could see how her partiality had ripped her house apart. Her biased attitude pitted her not only against Esau but also Isaac. She probably never thought her actions would have this outcome, especially since she thought she was just assisting God with what he told her when she was pregnant, "The older will serve the younger" (Genesis 25:23). Time was running out! Isaac was not well and had not blessed Jacob with the birthright he was due. In her desire to secure Jacob's future, she had driven them all completely apart.

Rebekah was a woman who had been blessed by God with a husband who loved both God and her. She had a life that many would have envied, but yet out of her own partiality and impatience, she destroyed her home with her own hands. Poor decision-making in families is a horrendous reality that happens daily around us. The book of Proverbs gives us encouragement on how to live with our family and how to interact with them so that we can have less heartbreak and more happily ever afters.

Delighting in God's Wisdom

The previous eight weeks of Proverbs have been designed to be studied chapter-by-chapter and verse-by-verse. However, a shift occurs in Solomon's writing in Chapter 10 which makes continuing to study in that manner difficult. Each of the prior nine chapters hung together under one topic such as wisdom, folly, morality, and the like, but now we find in chapters 10-30 all kinds of miscellaneous topics presented within every chapter and no common theme. Proverbs, as a whole, is a collection of brief statements of truth that are not necessarily to be considered promises but rather words for wise living. Therefore, Stacy and I will take you through Proverbs 10-30 by assigning a theme for each week and then pulling out the various Proverbs that fit the topic of study.

Our prayer for you is that the book of Proverbs will be a guidebook for specific areas of life. As we study through specific topics, we are going to encourage you to mark them with a letter or symbol in your Bible, so Proverbs can be used as an easy reference source in the future.

RECEIVING God's Word

Open in Prayer
Read: Proverbs 10:1, 12:4, 14:1, 16:31, 18:22, 19:13-14, 19:26, 21:9, 23:24-25.

As you read each verse, please place the letter "F" next to the verse in your Bible for future reference on family issues.

EXPERIENCING God's Word

Experience 1: The Wise Woman

1. Proverbs 14:1 says, "The wise woman builds her house, but the foolish pulls it down with her hands." Rewrite this Proverb in your own words and explain what it means.

2. Read Genesis 16:1-5. Abraham was given a promise by God concerning his future descendants. God told Abraham that through him a great nation would come. His wife, Sarai, knew that the heir would come through Abraham. She grew impatient waiting for the son of promise to be conceived as she watched herself age past her childbearing years. How did Sarai foolishly tear down her own home by taking matters into her own hands?

3. Proverbs 16:31 says, "The silver-haired head is a crown of glory, if it is found in the way of righteousness." Rewrite this Proverb in your own words and explain what it means.

    a. Why is the word "if" so important in this Proverb?

Delighting in God's Wisdom

4. Read Titus 2:1-5. Titus 2:2 refers to men, but verse 3 says the things listed in verse 2 also apply to the older women. List the Godly attributes of the wise, older woman. Explain why these attributes are beautiful at any age but are a crown of glory in the older woman.

   a. According to these verses, how do these attributes please God?

Experience 2: Relationship Between a Wife and her Husband

1. Proverbs 12:4 says, "An excellent wife is the crown of her husband, but she who causes shame is like rottenness to his bones." Rewrite this Proverb in your own words and explain what it means.

2. Read 1 Timothy 3:8-12. Paul is giving Timothy a list of qualifications for deacons and their wives. Regardless of whether or not your husband is a deacon, these are honorable qualities God desires in wives. List the qualities that Paul describes. Then write the opposite quality next to it and state how the behavior can cause "rottenness to a husband's bones."

   Qualities: Opposite behavior: Causes rottenness to his bones:

3. Proverbs 18:22 says, "He who finds a wife finds a good thing and obtains favor from the LORD." Rewrite this Proverb in your own words and explain what it means.

4. Read Genesis 2:18-20. According to God's creation, what is the role of the wife to her husband? How is this a "good thing?"

5. Proverbs 19:13b-14 says, "And the contentions of a wife are a continual dripping. Houses and riches are an inheritance from fathers, but a prudent wife is from the LORD." Rewrite this Proverb in your own words and explain what it means.

6. Proverbs 21:9 says, "Better to dwell in a corner of a housetop than in a house shared with a contentious woman." Rewrite this Proverb in your own words and explain what it means.

7. Read Colossians 3:16-18. What should our tone of voice and conversation be like in general, but specifically with our husbands according to these verses?

   a. How is this possible?

    b. What is the command given to wives?

Experience 3: Relationship Between a Woman and her Child

1. Proverbs 10:1 says, "A wise son makes a glad father, but a foolish son is the grief of his mother." Rewrite this Proverb in your own words and explain what it means.

2. Proverbs 19:26 says, "He who mistreats his father and chases away his mother is a son who causes shame and brings reproach." Rewrite this Proverb in your own words and explain what it means.

3. Proverbs 23:24-25 says, "The father of the righteous will greatly rejoice, and he who begets a wise child will delight in him. Let your father and your mother be glad and let her who bore you rejoice." Rewrite this Proverb in your own words and explain what it means.

4. Read Ephesians 6:1-3. Why is it important to instruct our children to obey their parents? What promise does God give to the child and the parents as well?

Experience 4: Rebekah
Read Genesis 24

In Genesis 24 we meet Rebekah. Abraham's son, Isaac, was the son God gave Sarah and Abraham in their old age. It would be through Isaac that God would bring forth the nation of Israel. Isaac was not yet married. Abraham sends one of his servants to a nearby well in hopes of finding the woman that God has planned for Isaac's future. The servant has a divine encounter with Rebekah who is described in Genesis 24:15-17. She is a virgin, of a family line that was appropriate, according to God's plan, and she was beautiful.

1. Read Genesis 25:21-28. Rebekah was barren, and Isaac asked the LORD to give her a child. She conceived but the babies seemed to be very active within her, causing her to seek the LORD. What did God say to her in verse 23 regarding the twins in her womb?

   a. From these verses, what do you learn about the two boys and their parents?

2. In Genesis 25:29-34 we learn that Jacob took advantage of his brother, Esau. Knowing Esau's weaknesses, Jacob offers Esau a stew in exchange for his birthright and Esau complies. Isaac loved Esau. One day, he asks Esau to hunt game for him and make him some savory food. Isaac told Esau he would then bless him before he dies. Read Genesis 27:5-17. How does Rebekah insert herself and Jacob into a situation that had nothing to do with them?

3. The plan works, and Isaac unknowingly blesses Jacob instead of Esau. When Esau comes back from the field, he learns what happened. Read Genesis 27:41-46. How do Esau and Rebekah respond?

   a. How has Rebekah acted unwisely as a wife and mother and, in turn, negatively influenced the family?

ACTING on God's Word

While Stacy and I were writing this week's study, many of the Proverbs and their personal application to my life were encouraging, but also convicting. For me (Brenda), I was encouraged when I read Proverbs 18:22 which says, "He who finds a wife finds a good thing and obtains favor from the LORD." I praise God that my husband, Mike, found me, and we have enjoyed God's favor.

Delighting in God's Wisdom

Yet, when I read Proverbs 19:13b which says, "And the contentions of a wife are a continual dripping," I was convicted a bit. I am sure there have been days I sounded more like an irritating, dripping faucet than a good gift to Mike. This is an area that I need to work on with the Lord's help. The visual of sounding like a dripping faucet is memorable, and I believe it will remind me, the next time I'm unhappy, that sounding like one is annoying!

Just as I have been encouraged and convicted through our lesson, I can only guess you have been too. For the next four weeks, the Acting portion in our study will guide you to think about which Proverb encouraged you, which convicted you, and what your response will be to what you have learned. Try the first one by filling in your thoughts below.

1. Proverbs _____:_____
    a. How does this Proverb encourage you? Explain.

2. Proverbs _____:_____
    a. How does this Proverb convict you? Explain.

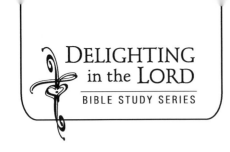

    b.   Is there a change God is leading you to make? Explain.

3. Where do you struggle within your family dynamics?

    a.   What can you apply from the verses in our lesson to your area of need?

 **D** **DELIGHTING** in God's Word

Reflecting back on our verses, how has the Lord prompted you to pray?

Write a verse that God has spoken to your heart.

Close in Prayer

"The one thing I ask of the Lord - the thing I seek most - is to live in the house of the Lord all the days of my life, delighting in the Lord's perfections and meditating in his temple." Psalm 27:4

WEEK 10
MONEY MATTERS

Selected Verses from Proverbs 10-30

She continued to awake each morning to the disbelief that her brother was still alive. She couldn't believe that he was raised back to life, in spite of the serious illness that led to his death just days before. Shock and awe overcame her as she relived the moments of him being raised to life; the moment Jesus cried out to God on behalf of her brother. The echo of His words still rang in her ears, "Lazarus, come forth!" (John 11:43) The vision of her brother walking out of the cave, wrapped in grave clothes with breath back in his lungs and strength in his legs was more than she could comprehend. It was unbelievable and yet true. He was alive for all to see! Jesus is the redeemer of all things, even life and death. She could never repay Him for this indescribable gift. She could never give back to Him what He had given to her. Deep gratitude filled her heart. The love she had for Jesus was overflowing from within. She was quickly brought back to reality as her sister, Martha, entered the room to tell her that she had heard Jesus was coming back to Bethany. With great zeal and enthusiasm, Martha suggested a supper be served in his honor. He had come to spend time with them as He passed through town. Plans were put into motion.

That night, Jesus dined with them as the disciples gathered, along with Lazarus, in Simon's house. The conversation was lively and the atmosphere was one of joy and celebration, and yet there was a seriousness to Jesus. She sensed something but couldn't quite put her finger on it. All she wanted to do was pour out her love to Jesus. She wanted Him to know how important He was to her. She didn't have much, but what she did have she would give to Him. She had slipped a tiny bottle of fragrant spikenard oil into her pocket earlier that day. As an act of worship, she would anoint His feet.

One could imagine that she meekly approached Jesus, not wanting to be disrespectful. Politely excusing herself, she asked Jesus if she could anoint His feet. The conversation stopped, and all eyes fell on her. She didn't care. She knelt down, cradling Jesus' feet in her hands, and poured the oil over his feet. She took her hair and wiped the oil from His feet, and at once the whole house smelled of spikenard. A hush filled the room only to be interrupted by Judas Iscariot's angry rebuke. "Why was this fragrant oil not sold for three hundred denarii and given to the poor?" (John 12:5) Jesus knew the intent of Judas' heart. He didn't really care about the poor; he only cared about his personal wealth and prosperity. Taking what wasn't his, Judas regularly robbed the money box. He was a thief also trying to rob both Mary and Jesus of this beautiful moment.

Jesus quickly quieted Judas by telling him to leave Mary alone. Her heart was one of humble giving. It was the kind of heart that Jesus adored. She knew her richness wasn't in the costly bottle of perfume. Her riches were in Jesus, and no amount of money could buy what only Jesus could give. All she had was His.

This week we will be looking at verses in Proverbs about money, wealth, and giving. Solomon was one of the richest men in the world during his time, but he also knew what it was like losing it all. He had a lot to say about riches and one's heart attitude in this area. There are over 100 Proverbs addressing this topic. Don't worry, we won't have you look at all of them! We've pulled a few that we believe summarize the main areas that can cause us trouble when it comes to money. 1 Timothy 6:10 says that "the love of money is a root of all kinds of evil, for which some have strayed from the faith in their greediness and pierced themselves through with many sorrows." I (Stacy) think we are all too well acquainted with the evil that can come with money when our hearts are not trusting in God first. God desires that our hearts are ruled by Him instead of money. May we be like Mary, who knew everything comes from God, and from that place of worship, give back to Him and His people.

RECEIVING God's Word

Open in Prayer
Read Proverbs 11:4, 11:24-25, 13:7, 15:16-17, 17:5a, 18:10-11, 22:2, 22:9, 23:4-5, 28:6

As you read each verse, please place a dollar sign "$" next to the verse in your Bible for future reference on money issues.

EXPERIENCING God's Word

Experience 1: Trusting in God, not Wealth

1. Proverbs 11:4 says, "Riches do not profit in the day of wrath, but righteousness delivers from death." Rewrite the Proverb in your own words and explain what it means.

2. Proverbs 18:10-11 says, "The name of the LORD is a strong tower; the righteous run to it and are safe. The rich man's wealth is his strong city, and like a high wall in his own esteem." Rewrite the Proverb in your own words and explain what it means.

3. Read Luke 21:1-4. How did the widow's offering demonstrate her trust in God?

Delighting in God's Wisdom

4. Read Mark 10:17-22. Contrast the rich young ruler's attitude toward money with the widow's attitude toward money.

Experience 2: Generous Giving

1. Proverbs 11:24-25 says, "There is one who scatters, yet increases more; and there is one who withholds more than is right, but it leads to poverty. The generous soul will be made rich, and he who waters will also be watered himself." Rewrite the Proverb in your own words and explain what it means.

2. Proverbs 22:9 says, "He who has a generous eye will be blessed, for he gives of his bread to the poor." Rewrite the Proverb in your own words and explain what it means.

3. Read 2 Corinthians 9:6-8. What connection is being made in these verses between giving and receiving?

   a. From these verses, how are we to give to the Lord?

   b. How does God reward generous giving?

Experience 3: *Love of Money*

1. Proverbs 13:7 says, "There is one who makes himself rich, yet has nothing; and one who makes himself poor, yet has great riches." Rewrite the Proverb in your own words and explain what it means.

2. Proverbs 23:4-5 says, "Do not overwork to be rich; because of your own understanding, cease! Will you set your eyes on that which is not? For riches certainly make themselves wings; they fly away like an eagle toward heaven." Rewrite the Proverb in your own words and explain what it means.

3. Read Matthew 6:19-21. We often fall into a trap regarding money. What is the trap and how does this verse give caution?

4. Read Matthew 6:33. What should we be seeking each day and why?

Experience 4: Contentment

1. Proverbs 15:16-17 says, "Better is a little with the fear of the LORD, than great treasure with trouble. Better is a dinner of herbs where love is, than a fatted calf and hatred." Rewrite the Proverb in your own words and explain what it means.

2. Read Hebrews 13:5-6. How do contentment, the fear of the Lord, and wealth go together?

   a. What promise is given in these verses that should help us be secure?

Experience 5: Heart Attitude Toward Money

1. Proverbs 22:2 says, "The rich and poor have this in common, the LORD is maker of them all." Rewrite the Proverb in your own words and explain what it means.

2. Proverbs 28:6 says, "Better is the poor who walks in his integrity than one perverse in his ways, though he be rich." Rewrite the Proverb in your own words and explain what it means.

3. Proverbs 17:5a says, "He who mocks the poor reproaches his Maker." Rewrite the Proverb in your own words and explain what it means.

4. Read James 2:1-5. What do these verses say about God's impartial heart?

   a. As a result, what is God's expectation of us toward the rich and the poor?

   b. Fill in the blank: Partiality toward those with money is _____.

Experience 6: Mary of Bethany
Read John 12:1-7

1. Read Luke 10:38-42. What do you learn about Mary of Bethany?

2. John 11 tells of the death of Lazarus who was Mary of Bethany's brother. Jesus raised Lazarus from the dead and a celebration dinner took place days later in Bethany, at Simon the Leper's house. Read John 12:1-3. What does Mary do at the dinner? What do her actions symbolize regarding her love of Jesus and her love of money?

3. In verses 4-6 Mary's actions anger one of the guests. Who is angry and why?

   a. Compare the actions and heart attitude of Mary and the angered guest regarding things of monetary value.

4. Read verse 7. How did Jesus esteem Mary's actions?

ACTING on God's Word

My (Stacy's) unhealthy relationship with money began early in life. Living with a single mom who became disabled from a brain aneurism, the necessities of life were barely covered. We lived outside a small town in New York without a car, very few luxuries, and rationed food. Heating our house was a challenge financially, so rooms were closed off in the winter to conserve what little heat we used. Because of her disability, my mom was forced to retire from teaching and to live on a strict budget. And yet, she continually sacrificed what little she had so that we girls could enjoy a few extras each month. My mom planned everything: the monthly menu, the monthly budget, monthly rides to the grocery store, and even rides for us to get to school activities. God always provided. I never felt like I didn't have enough, unless my eyes wandered to those around me. It was then that the discontentment would settle in, as well as a sense of entitlement.

My mom loved the Lord, and from her heart she gave readily back to Him. Out of the little she received each month from the government, she would immediately write a check to the church for 10%. To this day, she still does. Tithing was taken seriously. If money was ever gifted to us girls, we immediately had to put 10% into a small silver canister in a cabinet in the dining room. That money was given to a ministry my mom supported each year. Those early years of learning to tithe were impressionable, but not for good reasons. I learned to give out of obedience and not from a heart's response. A rebellious spirit as well as a self-reliant, self-centered attitude was quick to take up residence in me in this area.

I never liked being the poor girl, and that definition soon defined all aspects of my life as a girl and young woman. Money did matter to me, but in very unhealthy ways. It would be through many years and financial challenges that God would work selfishness and self-reliance out of me in this area. As my relationship with Him grew, my relationship with money began to change. Giving came from a heart that understood His grace. I have learned and come to appreciate that all that I have is His. Whether my bank account has little or has plenty, my reliance cannot be on me or my husband, but on the Lord. And above all, from all that God has given, it is my reasonable act of service to give to Him, no matter what. I have seen the blessing of giving over and over again. It has become an act of worship. These lessons haven't come easily, and I know there are more to learn. As I have been willing to learn, God has taught me. Money doesn't define me or rule over me; God does. Please take these verses and meditate on them. Let God meet you in this area and do the work that only He can do.

Take two Proverbs from the Experience Section and fill in their reference below. Then answer the questions that follow.

1. Proverbs _____:_____
    a. How does this Proverb encourage you? Explain.

2. Proverbs _____:_____

   a. How does this Proverb convict you? Explain.

   b. Is there a change God is leading you to make? Explain.

3. What is your greatest struggle regarding finances and money? What can you apply from the verses in our lesson to your area of need?

 **D** **DELIGHTING** in God's Word

Reflecting back on our verses, how has the Lord prompted you to pray?

Write a verse that God has spoken to your heart.

Close in Prayer

"The one thing I ask of the Lord - the thing I seek most - is to live in the house of the Lord all the days of my life, delighting in the Lord's perfections and meditating in his temple." Psalm 27:4

WEEK 11
SELF-CONTROL MATTERS
Selected Verses from Proverbs 10-30

Another month passed, and once again Hannah was reminded of her barrenness. A womb that should hold life but didn't. Deep heartache and sadness overcame her. It wasn't enough that her body constantly reminded her of her emptiness, but she had to watch her husband's other wife, Peninnah, continue to have children. Peninnah took every opportunity to flaunt her children in front of Hannah. Her words were harsh toward Hannah, and her actions constantly provoked her. This only invoked more pain and misery for Hannah.

Every day was a lesson in self-control as Hannah restrained her words and her thoughts of retaliation. It took great faith for Hannah to not crumble in despair and hopelessness. But Hannah knew that God was able to give her a child, and her hope in Him sustained her. Year after year she would make the annual journey to the tabernacle in Shiloh, just north of Jerusalem, and worship God during feast time. It was there that she would pour her heart out to God.

That day Hannah made her way to the tabernacle. In complete anguish, she felt the bitterness settling in her soul. Still, she prayed to the LORD as that was all she knew. Unbeknownst to her, Eli the priest was watching her. He assumed she was drunk from the way her lips moved. Rebuking her, he said, "Put your wine away from you!" (1 Samuel 1:14b). Despite her sorrowful spirit, Hannah showed her virtue by telling him of her sobriety and faith in God. Having compassion for her, Eli told her to "Go in peace, and the God of Israel grant your petition which you have asked of Him." (1 Samuel 1:17) God's peace filled her heart, and gave her the strength she needed to continue on while she waited for God to answer her plea for a child. It would be within that year that her request would be answered, and God would fill her womb with a son.

The Proverbs we are studying in this lesson speak of a life governed by God and led by the Holy Spirit. It is only through the Lord that a life of self-control is possible. Like Hannah, we too have many areas of life where self-control is needed; our choices, our plans, our emotions, and our conduct toward others. Like Hannah, it can be especially difficult when life's circumstances and the people around us try to bring out our worst and provoke us to sin. It is during these times that self-control and diligence are required in order to honor God in these areas, and we should be careful not to follow after the dictates of our emotions or our thoughts. God desires us to be wise women who live lives of diligence and discipline in all areas. Let's see what He has to say!

RECEIVING God's Word

Open in Prayer
Read Proverbs 14:16-17, 14:23, 15:9, 16:3, 16:17, 19:11, 20:1, 21:5, 23:29-32, 25:28, 29:11

As you read each verse, please place an "SC" next to the verse in your Bible for future reference on self-control issues.

EXPERIENCING God's Word

Experience 1: Be Virtuous

1. Proverbs 16:3 says, "Commit your works to the Lord, and your thoughts will be established." Rewrite the Proverb in your own words and explain what it means.

2. Proverbs 16:17 says, "The highway of the upright is to depart from evil; he who keeps his way preserves his soul." Rewrite the Proverb in your own words and explain what it means.

Week 11: Self-Control Matters

3. Proverbs 25:28 says, "Whoever has no rule over his own spirit is like a city broken down, without walls." Rewrite the Proverb in your own words and explain what it means.

4. Read Philippians 4:8. In order to have self-control over our thought life, it requires a choice that we put into action. What is that choice, according to this verse, and how do we walk it out?

5. Read 2 Peter 1:2-7. In these verses we are told diligence is needed for self-control. What is the progression that is given in verse 5?

    a. From these verses, explain how we are able to follow this progression. What enables us?

Experience 2: Be Sober

1. Proverbs 20:1 says, "Wine is a mocker, strong drink is a brawler, and who ever is led astray by it is not wise." Rewrite the Proverb in your own words and explain what it means.

2. Proverbs 23:29-32 says, "Who has woe? Who has sorrow? Who has contentions? Who has wounds without cause? Who has redness of eyes? Those who linger long at the wine, those who go in search of mixed wine. Do not look on the wine when it is red, when it sparkles in the cup, when it swirls around smoothly; At the last it bites like a serpent, and stings like a viper." Rewrite the Proverb in your own words and explain what it means.

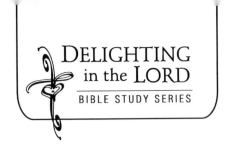

a. Read 1 Peter 5:8-9. Here we are told to "be sober and vigilant." What does this mean?

b. When we are hurting deeply and feeling the burden of life's trials, Proverbs 23:29-32 makes the point that some turn to alcohol. According to these verses in 1 Peter and Proverbs 23, how can alcohol be a tool used by Satan in our lives?

c. How does "being sober and vigilant" help in regards to the temptation to drink in excess?

3. Ephesians 5:18-19 gives us the answer on how to handle our emotions when we turn to alcohol to cover our pain. What is the answer?

Experience 3: Be Calm

1. Proverbs 14:16-17 says, "A wise man fears and departs from evil, but a fool rages and is self-confident. A quick-tempered man acts foolishly, and a man of wicked intentions is hated." Rewrite the Proverb in your own words and explain what it means.

2. Proverbs 19:11 says, "The discretion of a man makes him slow to anger, and his glory is to overlook a transgression." Rewrite the Proverb in your own words and explain what it means.

3. Proverbs 29:11 says, "A fool vents all his feelings, but a wise man holds them back." Rewrite the Proverb in your own words and explain what it means.

4. Read James 1:19. When engaged in conversation, speaking without really listening first can be dangerous and shows a lack of self-control that could lead to an angry response. How does this verse encourage you to handle conversations in a Godly way?

5. In Psalm 37:7-9, David gives us a few examples of things that can cause people to get angry. What are those things?

   a. What is David's answer for anger?

6. Read Ephesians 4:25-32. According to these verses, what is anger? How does it grieve the Holy Spirit?

   a. List all the ways we are to demonstrate self-control according to these verses.

    b. What should our actions be toward one another? How does this help us to be calm?

Experience 4: Be Diligent

1. Proverbs 14:23 says, "In all labor there is profit, but idle chatter leads only to poverty." Rewrite the Proverb in your own words and explain what it means.

2. Proverbs 15:19 says, "The way of the lazy man is like a hedge of thorns, but the way of the upright is a highway." Rewrite the Proverb in your own words and explain what it means.

3. Proverbs 21:5 says, "The plans of the diligent lead surely to plenty, but those of everyone who is hasty, surely to poverty." Rewrite the Proverb in your own words and explain what it means.

4. The verses in Proverbs tell us to be diligent in work, in conduct, and with our plans. Read Galatians 6:9. How is this verse an encouragement as we seek to be diligent in these areas?

   a. How does diligence require self-control?

5. Read Philippians 3:12-14 and 2 Peter 3:14. How does diligence come?

Experience 5: Hannah
Read 1 Samuel 1:1 through 2:11

1. In these verses we are introduced to a man named Elkannah. He had two wives named Peninnah and Hannah. Read 1 Samuel 1:1-7. Peninnah had children but Hannah didn't. How did Peninnah treat Hannah and what reasons are given for this unkindness?

2. Read 1 Samuel 1:8-16. How do you see Hannah responding to the provocations of Peninnah as well as her childless state?

3. Eli the priest watched Hannah as she was at the tabernacle praying. Read 1 Samuel 1:17-20. What did Eli say to Hannah in verse 17, and how was it fulfilled in verses 19-20?

4. Read 1 Samuel 1:21-28. How does Hannah continue to show self-control in her actions?

5. In 1 Samuel 2:1-11 we see Hannah's prayer to the Lord. Read her prayer. What do you learn about Hannah's heart from this prayer that gives insight into how she was able to exhibit such self-control with unkind people and very difficult situations?

ACTING on God's Word

Proverbs 25:28 says, "Whoever has no rule over his own spirit is like a city broken down, without walls." This Proverb is very convicting to me, Stacy. It creates such a picture in my mind of the collateral damage that can occur when we, as women, do not tend to the areas of our hearts while living undisciplined lives. I think a lot of us could look around and see "a city broken down." Why is this? What is it that is causing destruction in our homes, our marriages, and the lives of our family members? The only one we are truly responsible for is ourselves. We will stand before God one day and give an account to Him for all that we did in His name (1 Corinthians 3:11-13). How diligent were we to keep Him first in our lives and let all else flow from that place of love and submission?

Week 11: Self-Control Matters

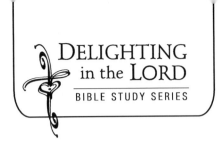

We live in a time when so much calls for our time and resources. How many times has someone asked, "How are you doing?" and your response is, "I'm so busy." We live in a culture where cell phones constantly interrupt daily moments in life. The media - especially social media - lures us into the prepackaged and filtered worlds of others that causes us to engage in idle chatter and wasted time. The TV promotes lifestyles of promiscuity, alcohol, and indulgent choices, telling us, "It's all about what feels good to me!" Living a life of self-control is not only hard, but exhausting…who needs it anyway? I do! You do! We all do if we are to live a life pleasing to God.

This past year I had a herniated disc in my lower back causing severe pain. Exercise has always been important to me and discipline in this area comes easier than in other areas. My back injury prohibited me from exercising and, as a result, I stopped showing self-control with food. It was a downward cycle. I have just recently started exercising again. Instead of looking at all I needed to do to get back to where I was pre-injury, I decided I would just focus on one step forward in fitness and health each day. One step; that's all it takes. One purposeful and prayerful step toward the goal. What step will you take today to build up the city that God has placed you in? You can do it by God's power and strength.

Take two Proverbs from today's verses and fill in their reference below. Then answer the questions that follow.

1. Proverbs _____ : _____
   a. How does this Proverb encourage you? Explain.

2. Proverbs _____:_____
   a. How does this Proverb convict you? Explain.

   b. Is there a change God is leading you to make? Explain.

3. What is your greatest struggle regarding self-control? What can you apply from the verses in our lesson to your area of need?

 **D DELIGHTING in God's Word**

Reflecting back on our verses, how has the Lord prompted you to pray?

Write a verse that God has spoken to your heart.

Close in Prayer

"The one thing I ask of the Lord - the thing I seek most - is to live in the house of the Lord all the days of my life, delighting in the Lord's perfections and meditating in his temple." Psalm 27:4

WEEK 12
THE MOUTH MATTERS

Selected Verses from Proverbs 10-30

I can imagine Huldah walking out of her home and looking around. The town was changing, and it was finally for the better! There was unity and hope among the people, which was a direct result of the leadership of King Josiah. He became the king of Judah at the young age of eight, but the first ten years of his leadership seemed to be more about preparing to lead rather than actually leading the people. However, now that Josiah was 18 years old, he was truly making a difference as king. One thing he was certainly getting right was drawing the people back to God. How different he was compared to the numerous kings who had previously sinned against God with their idol worship. As a woman who had consecrated herself to serving the Lord, Huldah welcomed the change after the damage done by King Josiah's wicked predecessors.

One of the biggest changes Huldah noticed recently was the restoration of the house of the Lord. It had fallen into disrepair, so King Josiah had hired masons, carpenters and builders to begin the very important and necessary job of reconstructing their place of worship. Interestingly, during the restoration process, the lost Book of the Law had been found! To Josiah's credit, he immediately had the Holy book read to him, but upon hearing its words he ripped his clothes in grief. The words convicted him because he recognized just how far the country of Judah had fallen from God's requirements for His people. Huldah wondered what the king would do now, considering what had been discovered.

As Huldah was replaying these events over in her mind, she noticed one of the king's servants coming up the road toward her home. What was he doing here in her part of town? Certainly, he was not coming to her home, or was he? Sure enough, after introducing himself, he explained he wanted her to inquire of the Lord on behalf of King Josiah, because the people of Judah had not followed the Book of the Law. With male prophets like Jeremiah and Zephaniah available to consult, did Huldah wonder why the king had picked her? She did not ask that question, but instead immediately began to pray.

The words that came to her were not good, but thankfully there was still some hope. Huldah breathed in, and then, with holy boldness, she spoke the words the Lord gave to her about what was coming for her country. She explained that calamity was surely coming to them as a nation, but God would be merciful during Josiah's lifetime. The servant listened intently. He then turned and left with the words he would have to share with Josiah. Hope and despair mingled in the air as Huldah watched him walk back toward the palace of the king. The people of Judah had been disobedient for so long that a correction was needed, but Huldah would continue to pray for God's mercy over the discipline which was still yet to come. (2 Kings 22:19-20)

Huldah was a woman who knew when to speak and when to be silent. She understood discernment, and trusted the Lord to communicate what she was to say and when. It appears that she may have understood Proverbs 18:21a, "Death and life are in the power of the tongue," before it was even written. Huldah knew the words she would repeat to the servant were life-giving, but yet certainly meant death to many people. She metered her words carefully, yet did not mince them. Thirty-five years later, the words of this prophetess would come true exactly as she said they would come to pass. Huldah is a good example of how to speak carefully, with the understanding that words have power, and we would be wise to utter them judiciously.

The book of James reminds us that our tongue is a small but powerful member of our body that is oh, so hard to control. Reading Proverbs will remind us of this true fact. Proverbs also reminds us to be aware of the damage we can do when we do not govern our tongue prudently. May your time of study be rich as you examine this topic and how it applies to everyday living. May we learn how we can successfully keep our mouth pleasing to the Lord when the power of the Holy Spirit is in control of our tongue.

RECEIVING God's Word

Open in Prayer

Read: Proverbs 10:18, 10:19, 12:22, 12:23, 15:1, 15:23, 16:24, 16:27-28, 17:9, 17:27, 20:3, 25:15.

As you read each verse, please place an "M" next to the verse in your Bible for future reference on matters related to our speech.

 **EXPERIENCING** God's Word

Experience 1: Speaking Gossip and Lies

1. Proverbs 10:18 says, "Whoever hides hatred has lying lips, and whoever spreads slander is a fool." Rewrite the Proverb in your own words and explain what it means.

2. Proverbs 12:22 says, "Lying lips are an abomination to the LORD, but those who deal truthfully are His delight." Rewrite the Proverb in your own words and explain what it means.

3. Proverbs 16:27-28 says, "An ungodly man digs up evil, and it is on his lips like a burning fire. A perverse man sows strife, and a whisperer separates the best of friends." Rewrite the Proverb in your own words and explain what it means.

4. Proverbs 17:9 says, "He who covers a transgression seeks love, but he who repeats a matter separates friends." Rewrite the Proverb in your own words and explain what it means.

5. Read James 3:2-11. Answer the following questions.

   a. According to verse 2, what is an area of stumbling for many people?

   b. In verses 3-6 the tongue is compared to three different things. What are they? Explain the comparison being made.

   c. Verses 7 and 8 give us further information about the tongue. What it is?

d. In verses 9-11 the tongue is behaving in a contradictory manner. Why is this a problem?

Experience 2: Speaking Kindness and Love

1. Proverbs 15:1 says, "A soft answer turns away wrath, but a harsh word stirs up anger." Rewrite the Proverb in your own words and explain what it means.

2. Proverbs 15:23 says, "A man has joy by the answer of his mouth, and a word spoken in due season, how good it is!" Rewrite the Proverb in your own words and explain what it means.

3. Proverbs 16:24 says, "Pleasant words are like a honeycomb, sweetness to the soul and health to the bones." Rewrite the Proverb in your own words and explain what it means.

4. Proverbs 25:15 says, "By long forbearance a ruler is persuaded, and a gentle tongue breaks a bone." Rewrite the Proverb in your own words and explain what it means.

5. Read 2 Timothy 2:23-24. What two things are we told to avoid and why?

   a. In verse 24 a servant of the Lord is being addressed specifically. What do the words of a servant of the Lord look like?

6. Read Colossians 4:6. What does graceful speech sound like and what does speech seasoned with salt sound like?

   a. In your own words give an example of how you would phrase each type of speech.

Experience 3: Silence and Restraint

1. Proverbs 10:19 says, "In the multitude of words sin is not lacking, but he who restrains his lips is wise." Rewrite the Proverb in your own words and explain what it means.

2. Proverbs 12:23 says, "A prudent man conceals knowledge, but the heart of fools proclaims foolishness." Rewrite the Proverb in your own words and explain what it means.

3. Proverbs 17:27 says, "He who has knowledge spares his words, and a man of understanding is of a calm spirit." Rewrite the Proverb in your own words and explain what it means.

4. Proverbs 20:3 says, "It is honorable for a man to stop striving, since any fool can start a quarrel." Rewrite the Proverb in your own words and explain what it means.

5. Read Mark 15:1-5. As Jesus stands before Pilate, false accusations come against Him, and He behaves in an unusual way. Explain his behavior.

    a. What do you learn from Jesus' behavior regarding when to speak and when to be silent?

6. Read Galatians 5:16. Explain what we need in order to be victorious in the areas of exercising restraint in our speech.

Experience 4: Huldah
Read 2 Kings 22

1. Read 2 Kings 22:1-2. List all you learn about Josiah.

2. Josiah decides to repair the temple. Many of the kings before him were evil and did not honor God or His law. Josiah was different. Read verses 3-8. What is found in the house of the LORD during the time of the repairs?

3. In verses 9-13, why is Josiah so upset and what is his command?

4. Tensions were high. The king was very upset and he needed answers. There were many prophets his men could have turned to, and yet they go to Huldah, the Prophetess, who served at the same time as Jeremiah and Zephaniah. Read 2 Kings 22:14-17. What does she say concerning the people and the kingdom of Judah?

5. Read 2 Kings 22:18-20. What does Huldah say regarding King Josiah?

6. How did Huldah's words demonstrate a woman of wisdom?

 **ACTING on God's Word**

If you have not met me (Brenda), you may not know that I am an extrovert; gregarious, transparent, friendly, and fun-loving. I am typically energized when I am around other people and can talk to almost anyone, even complete strangers in a grocery store. How about you?

There is nothing inherently wrong with these character traits except when I occasionally feel like I've either talked too much or have said more than was necessary. I find this happens most often when I'm excited about a topic being discussed, or I've had too much caffeine. Knowing my tendencies in this area of my life, I have a reminder located in the front of my Bible which I have turned into a regular prayer. It says, "May I listen more and talk less." This is a lofty goal for me. Yet, based on what we have learned in our study this week, it is worthy and necessary to work toward it because it is exercised regularly by wise women. That is what stood out to me from the lesson.

Take two Proverbs from today's verses and fill in their reference below. Then answer the questions that follow.

1. Proverbs _____:_____
   a. How does this Proverb encourage you? Explain.

2. Proverbs _____:_____
   a. How does this Proverb convict you? Explain.

b. Is there a change that God is leading you to make? Explain.

c. How will you plan to implement the changes you feel God is challenging you to make?

D DELIGHTING in God's Word

Reflecting back on our verses, how has the Lord prompted you to pray?

Write a verse that God has spoken to your heart.

Close in Prayer

"The one thing I ask of the Lord - the thing I seek most - is to live in the house of the Lord all the days of my life, delighting in the Lord's perfections and meditating in his temple." Psalm 27:4

WEEK 13
THE WISE WOMAN: MS. 31

Proverbs 31

She is nameless, but certainly doesn't go unnoticed. Her reputation has honored her throughout succeeding generations, and I'm sure you've heard of her too. She is a valuable treasure, not only to her husband but to her family and community. She lives for God, and her attitude and actions follow from a heart set first on Him. She joyfully fulfills her role as wife and mother in the everyday, often mundane activities of making meals, clothing her family, and tending to her home. And yet, she is also industrious, charitable, and a keen business woman. She looks out for the interests of others before herself; those around her feel safe, especially her husband.

She rises early and goes to bed late. She diligently meets the needs of her family. At the same time, she also takes care of herself. She tends to her appearance and gives careful attention to her relationship with God. It is the well-spring of her life. From that well, dug deep in the Lord, comes kindness, strength, discernment, and above all, wisdom. She knows her priorities and is disciplined to keep to them. She is praised by many and lacks nothing.

Is this woman for real?

Throughout our study on Proverbs, we've looked at many women in order to learn from their wise and unwise examples. We will finish with this woman, who we are calling Ms. 31. She is a married woman, but we chose Ms. because any woman can walk in these desirable personality traits, whether she is married or single. It's never too early to pursue becoming a woman who reflects these Godly virtues. Over time she has been held up as the "ideal woman." The world wants to define the ideal woman as one who is airbrushed, touched up, power-driven and self-focused. Ms. 31 is anything but that. She is our model, yet not the one the world would put on magazine covers and TV screens.

In Proverbs 31, a mother teaches her son what to look for in a woman. This woman is beautiful inside and out. She is an example of a powerful woman who is under the control of the Holy Spirit. She is faithful to her calling as a wife and mother. In that calling, she is content using her sphere of influence to affect those around her for good. She actively participates in the affairs of her family and community.

Her example for us should be an encouragement; not a condemnation. Yet, we can read Ms. 31's attributes and description and think we just can't measure up. We have to guard our hearts against comparison. I (Stacy) pray, as you study Proverbs 31, you will focus on where God wants to take you to further refine you, whether as a wife, a mother, or a single person. We may look at Ms. 31 and say, "I'll never be a woman who doesn't raise her voice." Instead, may we say, "Lord, help me to be a woman filled with the Spirit of self-control, like I see in Ms. 31." Maybe you say, "I'll never be content with laundry, dishes, or diapers." Instead, may we say, "thank you Lord for allowing me this opportunity to care for my family." May Ms. 31 be an inspiration and someone we desire to emulate. May she be a testimony to us of all that is possible under God's hand.

No matter your season of life: single, married, mother, or grandmother; when we read of Ms. 31, may we let it be our prayer that God would do His work in each of us, the work that is needed for us to be wise and virtuous women. May Ms. 31 not be just the woman we read about in Scripture, but may we be a Ms. 31. Above all, may we seek to live a life pleasing to God, knowing "a woman who fears the LORD, she shall be praised." (Proverbs 31:30b)

R   RECEIVING God's Word

Open in Prayer
Read Proverbs 31

E   EXPERIENCING God's Word

1. Read Proverbs 31:1-10. Verse 10 begins with a rhetorical question. Why do you think King Lemuel would begin a passage about the ideal woman, who we will refer to as Ms. 31, in this way?

    a. Define the word virtuous.

    b. How is value assigned to the woman described in verse 10? How would you assign value to this woman in modern-day terminology?

> "The woman described in the rest of the chapter is rare and valuable, but her value is greater than what she does as explained in the following verses in Proverbs 31. Her value or worth should not be reduced to the performance of these qualities; she will be virtuous before she acts in a virtuous manner." (David Guzik, Blue Letter Bible commentary from Enduring Word)

2. Read Proverbs 31:11-12 and describe what has been entrusted to Ms. 31.

    a. Explain how her actions toward her husband demonstrate selflessness.

    b. How has the husband benefitted from her care?

3. Read Proverbs 31:13-24 and answer the following questions. Describe some of the jobs Ms. 31 undertakes. (List the jobs as they are given in these verses.)

   a. How are these jobs similar to things women do today? Take each job/task and describe a modern-day example. Write the jobs and examples below.

   b. Consider the character traits needed to do these jobs well. Write the character traits below that you see in these verses.

   c. From these verses, write down the descriptive words that speak to Ms. 31's attitude. Overall, what is her attitude in the different responsibilities she handles?

4. From verses 13-24, list all the groups of people she serves regularly. What does this say about her?

   a. Describe how Ms. 31 contributes to her community in these verses.

   b. How do you see Ms. 31 handling finances and being a financial contributor in her home and community in these verses?

5. Read Ephesians 5:22-24. How is a wife commanded by God to live in relationship to her husband?

   a. How do you see Ms. 31 obey Ephesians 5:22-24? Explain.

6. Read Proverbs 31:17, 22 and 25-30. How do you see Ms. 31 adorned?

   a. Read 1 Peter 3:3-6 and 1 Timothy 2:8-10. How is a Godly woman's adornment described? Does Ms. 31 fulfill this description? Explain.

7. Strength can be seen very differently by the world's standard and God's standard. What is the difference in the two views?

   a. To better understand God's view, read Philippians 4:13, 2 Corinthians 12:9-10 and Isaiah 40:29-31. How does a wise woman know how to use strength when seeking to live for God?

8. Read Genesis 2:18. What role did God give a wife?

a. Read Proverbs 31:10-31. How do you see Ms. 31 fulfilling this role?

9. Read Proverbs 31:26. How would you describe Ms. 31's speech?

10. Read Proverbs 31:27. What is Ms. 31's daily focus? How do you know her attention is focused on her role?

   a. In verse 27, the word for "watches" is the Hebrew word tsaphah. It means to lean forward, to peer into the distance and observe. The word for "ways" is haliykah. It defines walking with a caravan; a march or procession. Given these definitions, describe how Ms. 31 is attentive to her household.

11. Read Proverbs 31:28-31 and answer the following questions.

   a. What impact does she have on her family?

b. Along with verse 30, read Proverbs 1:7. Describe how Ms. 31 is wise. Is her wisdom in what she does and/or who she is? Explain.

c. According to verses 28-31, how does Ms. 31 get rewarded for her wisdom and virtue?

12. From what you learned, write a brief description of who Ms. 31 is in today's terminology. (ie. We don't put our hand to the distaff, but how would you describe this today?)

 **ACTING on God's Word**

I (Stacy) grew up in a broken home; broken in more ways than one. I am the daughter of a mom who became handicapped from a brain aneurism when I was three. My dad and mom divorced when I was six. Even though my mom was a believer, due to her brain injury she had many deficits to overcome as a mother, both physically and mentally. She definitely did her best and was, in her own way, a Proverbs 31 woman. And yet, I didn't have the example of a Godly marriage or the Proverbs 31 woman as portrayed in the verses we just studied. For Brenda, her mother, Carrie, embodied the woman described in Proverbs 31. Whereas her mother wasn't perfect, as none of our mothers are (nor are we); some of us are given a Godly earthly example and some are not.

Let's apply what we learned this week about Ms. 31, who is the wise and virtuous woman.

1. When you read the description of Ms. 31, what were your first thoughts about her?

2. What were your thoughts about yourself? How has the enemy used these thoughts to possibly discourage or defeat you?

3. From Ms. 31's complete description, what stood out to you the most?

4. How is God's standard of the "ideal woman" different from the world's standard?

5. How does Ms. 31's example bring conviction to you? What areas of your life can you pinpoint as areas that need God's sanctification/refinements?

6. How does Ms. 31's example encourage you? Explain.

7. If a young woman came to you asking for advice about having a Godly marriage and being a mother who honors God, what advice would you give her based on Proverbs 31?

8. We learned in our study of Proverbs that wisdom comes from a life that fears God and desires to know Him, learn from Him, and obey Him. What are some practical ways you can cultivate your relationship with God?

9. From your study of Proverbs, list three Proverbs and/or principles that stood out to you.

   a. How has the study of Proverbs impacted your life in Christ?

 **DELIGHTING in God's Word**

Reflecting back on our chapter, how has the Lord prompted you to pray?

 Write a verse from the chapter that God has spoken to your heart.

Close in Prayer

"The one thing I ask of the Lord - the thing I seek most - is to live in the house of the Lord all the days of my life, delighting in the Lord's perfections and meditating in his temple." Psalm 27:4

BIBLIOGRAPHY

"Free Bible Commentary from Pastor David Guzik." *Enduring Word*, enduringword.com

Ironside, H.A. *Notes on the Book of Proverbs*. Loizeaux Brothers, Inc., 1908. Republished edition, CrossReach Publications, 2017.

Phillips, John. *Exploring Proverbs: An Expository Commentary*. Kregel Publications, 2002.

Radmacher, Earl D., et al. *Nelsons NKJV Study Bible: NKJV, New King James Version*. T. Nelson, 2007.

Walvoord, John F., and Roy B. Zuck. *The Bible Knowledge Commentary: An Exposition of the Scriptures*. Victor, an Imprint of Cook Communications Ministries, 2004.

Wiersbe, Warren W. *Be Skillful: God's Guidebook to Wise Living: OT Commentary: Proverbs*. David C. Cook, 2009.

www.blueletterbible.com

Made in the USA
Middletown, DE
03 September 2019